An Ancient Land

THE YOUNG OXFORD HISTORY OF
BRITAIN & IRELAND

An Ancient Land

Prehistory ~ Vikings

MIKE CORBISHLEY

General Editor
PROFESSOR KENNETH O. MORGAN

OXFORD
UNIVERSITY PRESS

OXFORD
UNIVERSITY PRESS

Great Clarendon Street, Oxford OX2 6DP

Oxford University Press is a department of the University of Oxford.
It furthers the University's objective of excellence in research, scholarship,
and education by publishing worldwide in

Oxford New York

Athens Auckland Bangkok Bogotá Buenos Aires
Cape Town Chennai Dar es Salaam Delhi Florence Hong Kong Istanbul
Karachi Kolkata Kuala Lumpur Madrid Melbourne Mexico City Mumbai
Nairobi Paris São Paulo Shanghai Singapore Taipei Tokyo Toronto Warsaw

with associated companies in Berlin Ibadan

Oxford is a registered trade mark of Oxford University Press
in the UK and in certain other countries

First published 2001
Some material in this book was previously published in
The Young Oxford History of Britain & Ireland 1996

British Library Cataloguing in Publication Data available

Paperback ISBN 0–19–910828-5

1 3 5 7 9 10 8 6 4 2

Designed by Richard Morris, Stonesfield Design
Printed in China by Imago

CONTENTS

❖

CHAPTER 1

Ice, sea and land

❖

Many, many thousands of years ago Britain and Ireland were joined to the huge continent of Europe by low-lying land. For long periods, perhaps a thousand years at a time, large areas of Europe were covered by vast white sheets of ice, which is why this period in the history of Britain and Ireland is known as the Ice Ages. As the temperature fell, the sea froze into ice sheets. This does not mean that the whole of Europe was covered in a blanket of solid ice for all that time. But on about eight occasions parts of Britain and Ireland were completely uninhabitable, buried under ice hundreds of metres deep. During these very cold periods sea-water was locked up in ice sheets which joined Britain to Europe.

During those times when parts of Britain were completely uninhabitable, the landscape may have looked like this

As parts of Britain were first covered in ice and then freed from ice; as vegetation grew and animals appeared, the landscape and the coastline changed dramatically. Each time the ice covered the countryside, it destroyed the traces of earlier landscapes and peoples.

Many thousands of years ago Britain was part of Europe. For about 700,000 years the two were joined by low-lying land which for long periods at a time was covered by vast sheets of ice.

This map shows the coastline and ice coverage of about 10,000 years ago.

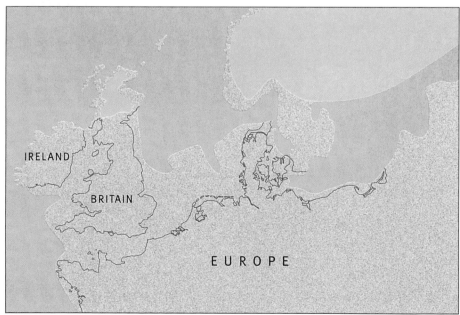

IRELAND

BRITAIN

EUROPE

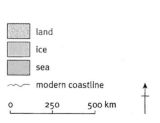

land

ice

sea

modern coastline

0   250   500 km

A changing landscape

The land on the edge of the ice sheets had very little living on it. On the tundra landscape (partly frozen landscape with little vegetation) further from the ice lived animals such as reindeer, woolly rhinoceros, mammoth and cave bears. The landscape which had been flattened and eroded by glaciers changed gradually in the warmer periods. It did not suddenly become warm. At first grasses, sedges and lichen grew on the land. Heathland shrubs were followed by hardy trees such as pine and birch. Then other trees such as oak began to grow.

Just as different animals can be found in different habitats today, so there were changes in the sorts of animals living in these changing landscapes. At first the giant deer and ox lived on an open landscape. As the grasslands changed to dense forests, animals such as wild boar and roe deer began to appear. At times it was warmer than it is in Britain today and elephant, hippopotamus, rhinoceros, red deer and hyena roamed the land.

At different times during the earliest periods in the history of the British Isles, the change in temperature brought changes to the landscape. This is an impression of the coast of South Wales about 120,000 years ago, during a warm period in August between glaciations. In early summer in the same place, but during an ice age, the vegetation would have been quite different, with small plants such as purple saxifrage, dwarf willow and lichens.

The first people in Britain

It is curious to think that the first people to see Britain must have walked across what is now the English Channel and the North Sea about 500,000 years ago. It was a warm period, but Britain was not completely cut off from Europe. The people who came were not our modern human species (we are called *homo sapiens sapiens*) but an early form of people called *homo erectus*. They were a little shorter on average than we are today and had heavier jaws and eyebrow ridges.

Homo erectus lived by hunting animals and gathering wild fruits, nuts and plants which they could eat. Small bands, each of about twenty-five people, followed herds of animals to hunt. Sometimes they settled and made a camp for the summer. Remains found at the sites of these camps show that gradually, as it became warmer, the bands of people moved further north.

In May 1994 national newspapers reported on an extraordinary find in a quarry at Boxgrove, near Chichester in Sussex. It was the shin bone of a man at least 500,000 years old. The archaeologists who found the remains called him 'the earliest European'. Archaeological excavations at the site showed that the bone came from a man (because of its size) and ridges on the bone show that he had good muscles. He was probably a good runner, and he needed to be because he was probably around 1.8 metres tall and weighed about 82.5 kilograms.

8 / HOME

THE INDEPENDENT

Sussex site yields oldest human find in Britain

DAVID KEYS
Archaeology Correspondent

THE OLDEST human remains to be found in Britain have been unearthed in a Sussex quarry.

Dating from between 520,000 and 480,000 years ago, the find is of immense importance to anthropologists — that period represents the time during which early humans, *Homo Erectus*, were evolving into an early type of more modern humans, archaic *Homo Sapiens*.

The bone — a tibia, or lower leg bone — is the largest of its type found anywhere. It has a circumference of 10.5cms, some 3cms more than the average modern man and over 1.5cms more than the average Neanderthal. The

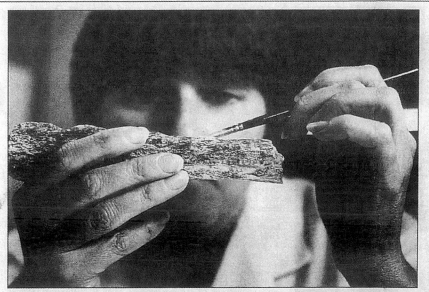

Lorraine Cornish, of the Natural History Museum, working on the bone *Photograph: Kayte Brmacombe*

This drawing shows what archaeologists think to be the evolution of people, from their origins in Africa to the present day. The people at Boxgrove have been identified with an earlier form of humans, somewhere between homo erectus *and modern people.*

| *Australopithecus* | *Homo habilis* | *Homo erectus* | *Boxgrove man* | *Neanderthal human* | *Modern human* |

Archaeologists found other evidence besides this bone. There were flint tools and animal bones. This hunter probably lived in a group of about fifteen to twenty-five people. Their main source of food was the animals which roamed the grasslands around, such as rhinoceros, bison, elephant, ancestors of the horse, and several different species of deer. We know something about the landscape too. Boxgrove is now ten kilometres inland but these early hunters camped on a sandy beach under a cliff.

Later, a different type of people arrived in Britain. These were similar to us and called *homo sapiens neanderthalensis* (the Neanderthal people). *Homo sapiens sapiens* appeared in Europe around 40,000 years ago.

Finding shelter

At one of the earliest places in which people lived in Britain there is now a golf course and a seaside pier! Hunting people came to what is now Clacton-on-Sea in Essex about 250,000 years ago. They made their camps on the banks of a river and hunted bison, deer, horses, elephants and rhinoceros. Archaeologists have found some of their tools, including flint choppers and tools for cutting up meat and cleaning animal skins. We know they had wooden tools as the tip of a spear, probably for thrusting not throwing, was one remarkable discovery.

Sometimes they lived in the entrances to caves. For example, a band of hunters lived in the Pontnewydd Cave in Clwyd, North Wales about 230,000 years ago. In Somerset and Devon several caves have been excavated to reveal the remains of these early hunting peoples. About 30,000 years ago the hunters left behind the remains of flint and bone tools and the bones of animals such as reindeer, Arctic fox, woolly rhinoceros and mammoth at Kent's Cavern near Torquay in Devon.

Archaeological excavations in progress at Pontnewydd Cave in Clwyd, North Wales. Archaeologists need to make a careful record of each find. Bones, including teeth, were found in the cave, which shows that Neanderthal people lived here for a time.

(right) People made tools and weapons from flint for tens of thousands of years. It took great skill to make these two tools, which are about half a million years old. They were held in the hand and used as all-purpose tools to cut and chop.

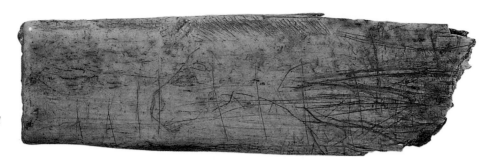

This engraving of a horse's head on a rib bone was found at Robin Hood's Cave in Derbyshire.

Ceremonies and beliefs

Just as we do today, these people clearly took some care in burying their dead. They may even have held special ceremonies for them. Exciting evidence of these early hunters comes from the cave called Goat's Cave in Paviland, South Wales. Between about 25,000 and 18,000 years ago a man was buried in the cave. With him were about fifty rods made from mammoth tusk, two ivory bracelets and two small piles of shells which once might have been in the pocket of his clothes, or in a bag.

His grave was shallow and the body had been sprinkled with red ochre. Ochre is an oxide of iron and occurs naturally. In early prehistoric times people used it as a paint, especially on cave walls. We know that they decorated bodies with it too, perhaps to give an impression of life to a corpse during the burial ceremony.

We have other information about the way of life and death of the early hunters in Britain. Evidence of the work of artists is still preserved among the objects discovered in a number of caves. Some pieces have scratch marks on bone which might have been a way of keeping a score or accounts. Others show real 'pictures' such as the engraving of a horse's head from Robin Hood's Cave in Derbyshire. Nothing that has been found in Britain is as spectacular as the cave-paintings from Lascaux in France or Altamira in Spain but all the drawings were made by similar hunting peoples. The most remarkable discovery of cave paintings was made in 1994 at Vallon-Pont-d'Arc in the Ardèche region of France, where hundreds of paintings were found in perfect condition, undisturbed since they were painted about 20,000 years ago.

Living in the wildwood

About 17,000 years ago the climate in Britain gradually began to change for good. The ice retreated from the south of the country and the glaciers began to melt. Slowly more people and animals moved to Britain from Europe, across the land which joined them together. These hunters spread through northern Britain, and west to what is now Wales, and they crossed to Ireland either over bridges in the land or in dug-out canoes. Over the next 10,000 years the landscape changed. Wildwoods of pine and birch covered large areas. Over thousands of years the

A camp dating from about 10,000 years ago at Mount Sandel in County Derry, Ireland. It was built by a group of about ten hunters. They built egg-shaped huts, made out of wooden posts pushed into the ground and lashed together.

In this photograph, on the left, part of the outside wall of the hut is shown by the holes left in the ground where wooden posts once stood. The hunters may have used skins or reeds to cover the frame and keep out the rain. They probably built a new one each year.

Inside and around the huts the remains of animals (tamed wolf, hare, wild pig), fish (salmon, trout and eel), birds (thrush, pigeon, black goose), hazelnuts and edible water lily all show that the hunters had a varied diet, and although there are no traces of berries or roots there must have been plenty of these around for them to eat.

wildwood transformed the landscape and with it the way of life of the hunters. None of that woodland remains today.

The hunters needed to adapt to these changes. No longer could they hunt large animals on open grassland plains. As their prey moved into the woods, they had to find new ways of hunting and killing. Their new weapons were spears, and bows and arrows. The tips of these hunting weapons were made from very small flint points, made with great skill. They also made axes and began to cut down trees, build shelters and make tools.

Some hunters set up their camps by lakes and lived by fishing as well as hunting. The best evidence we have for an encampment beside a lake is at Star Carr in North Yorkshire. The lake has long since disappeared but it was there nearly 11,000 years ago. The remains of a wooden paddle shows that the hunters must have had a boat, perhaps a dug-out canoe or a skin boat. They made a platform jutting out into the lake, which they used to reach their boats. On the bank near the platform, they built shelters out of wood and reeds. About three or four families (perhaps twenty-five people in all) probably lived here during the winter months and then spent the summer following herds of deer on the moors.

All sorts of bones have been found at Star Carr which show that these hunters lived on a great variety of animals, birds and fish; remains have been found of wild pig, red deer, wild cattle, elk, fox, pine marten, crane, grebe, lapwing, duck and white stork. There were some remains of a domesticated wolf, which perhaps provides the earliest evidence of a hunting companion found in Britain.

To these hunting people the deer was immensely important. We know this for two reasons. First, they would kill the stags (the males) rather than hinds (the females) or young. They probably wanted to make sure new deer would be born to keep up their regular supply of food. Second, the people of Star Carr took the skulls of stags to make head-dresses. They hollowed out part of the skull and cut out eye holes. They could have been worn to decoy deer to kill them or, more likely, in hunting ceremonies.

(right) A stag's skull from Star Carr. They cut holes in the skull, probably to attach it to a hood or cap, as part of a hunting ceremony or to decoy animals. You can see two of the four holes which were cut.

(below) Evidence gathered by archaeologists at Star Carr has been used to put together a picture of the hunters' camp around 9000 years ago.

From about 9000 years ago hunting groups moved north to sites in Scotland. At Morton, on the east coast of Scotland, archaeologists found the remains of wooden huts similar to those built at Mount Sandel. They worked out that between 8000 and 6000 years ago a group of hunters occupied a camp there. Around the huts were piles of food refuse, which are now called middens. Thousands of shells and crab pieces were found and bones from birds such as gannets, razorbills, cormorants and guillemots. The people at Morton must have had boats as they caught cod, salmon, sea trout and haddock. They also hunted on land for animals such as wild pig, deer and wild cattle.

An island people

By 8500 years ago or 6500 BC, Britain and Ireland had become islands in the North Atlantic Ocean, cut off from the mainland of Europe, and each other, by large areas of sea. We do not know how many people lived in these islands. Some archaeologists estimate 20,000 or more. There were certainly enough animals to hunt and plants to eat to support many more people than that.The sites which have been found suggest that they had moved west to Ireland and Wales, north to Scotland and east into Kent. By this time some groups of these hunting, fishing and food-gathering people had their own territory to work and probably did not travel very far. Some were still nomadic, moving from place to place for at least part of the year, but people were beginning to have an impact on the landscape. They cut down, or burnt down, trees; they managed herds of deer. They were almost farming.

These hunting peoples were far from primitive. There is plenty of evidence to show for example not only that they made and used their tools from flint and wood with skill, but also that they had proper burials and hunting ceremonies. All of this suggests that they were people who had an organised way of life, who thought about something more than just gathering food to survive. This is, however, the prehistoric period – there are no written records to help us guess at what they thought. We can only make interpretations from the surviving evidence.

CHAPTER 2

The first farmers

❖

In the lands of the Near East, from the Red Sea to the Persian Gulf, the idea of farming developed around 10,000 BC, at the end of the Ice Ages. People began to cultivate wild grasses as crops. They herded wild animals and then tamed them for breeding. Goats were the first to be tamed, then sheep, pigs and cattle were all domesticated.

This revolutionary idea of farming spread into other areas of the world as people moved and learnt from each other. In the following centuries many hunting peoples became farmers. By about 4000 BC farming peoples were looking for new lands in which to settle, building villages and cultivating the land all over northern Europe.

Around 4500 BC some European farming groups had crossed the sea and begun to settle in southern England and in Ireland. Although some hunting peoples were already taming wild cattle and pigs, we know that the new farming peoples brought sheep and other animals with them to Britain. Archaeologists have found the remains of many domesticated cattle and pigs. The bones of these animals are smaller than those of wild ones.

There were no cereal crops, such as wheat and barley, growing wild in Britain as there were in the Near East. These new crops were introduced by the immigrant farmers, who grew two sorts of wheat – emmer wheat and einkorn wheat. This wheat was their main crop but they also grew a sort of barley.

Slowly the huge forests gave way to these farming peoples as they cleared areas for their settlements. We do not know if they clashed with the hunters already there. Evidence shows that the hunting people had started to tame some animals. We know that they had tamed the wolf which they may have used to round up and herd wild cattle and pigs, but

Some animals continued to be hunted by the first farmers but other animals, such as this sheep, were domesticated.

they needed the forests for that was where the wild animals lived; farmers needed open country. Gradually the hunters copied and learnt from the farmers, tamed more animals and began to live off the land. By 3500 BC there were different kinds of peoples who lived in Britain and Ireland; the hunters and gatherers, and the early farmers.

Changing the landscape

The land to which the first farmers came was covered in forests. In southern Britain the trees in these forests were mainly oak, elm, hazel and alder, while in the north they were mainly birch and pine. The climate was warmer and wetter than it is today, which gave the farmers a longer growing period for their crops.

A farmer who grew crops needed a plough and something to pull it. The training and breeding of oxen must have been extremely important for these farmers.

These cattle or oxen are called 'Bos longifrons', and were used by the earliest European farmers. They were strong and bred specially for pulling a plough called an ard. This was a simple wooden plough which cut a furrow across a field, breaking up the soil as it went. The early farmers used the axe and the ard for clearing and cultivating the land.

The hunters had already begun to change the landscape by clearing parts of the forest for their temporary settlements. The new farmers probably made use of these clearings and destroyed yet more of the forest to make more space for their crops and animals. Disease may also have changed the landscape. Dutch Elm disease, which destroyed so many trees in Britain in the 1970s, may have destroyed some forest.

In building up a picture of how these early people lived, analysis of different kinds of pollen can provide a lot of detail. Pollen is a powdery substance found in any plants or trees which flower. Under a microscope it is possible to see individual pollen grains. Luckily pollen survives very well if trapped in places such as peat bogs. By identifying the different kinds of pollen from different plants archaeologists can tell where farmers cleared large areas of landscape. They can also see that this landscape was very different from the one which existed before the farmers arrived.

Settlements and villages

By 3000 BC remains found by archaeologists show that the farmers had spread out over the whole of Britain and Ireland. No longer pioneers, they were in charge of the land, building permanent settlements. They made houses out of wood or stone where it was available.

In the winter of 1850 there was a great storm in the Bay of Skaill in the bleak Orkney islands which lie off the north coast of Scotland. When it was over the astonishing sight of a complete farming village at Skara Brae on the island of Orkney Mainland was revealed. It was the first time it had been seen since about 2000 BC. The storm had blown away the sand dunes which covered the village.

The people of Skara Brae were farmers, but they also fished. The food refuse heaped up between the buildings, around the outside and on the roofs, contained plenty of evidence of farming (bones of cattle, sheep, pigs and dogs as well as seeds of crops); hunting (bones of deer and birds) and fishing (bones of codfish, shells of crabs and limpets).

In some parts of Britain the farmers built larger, more substantial settlements. These were

The windswept village at Skara Brae had about nine houses and a workshop. The extraordinary thing about the village, as this photograph shows, is that all the houses were built partly below ground, either alongside each other or connected by low, narrow passageways. This gave the villagers some protection, both from the weather and from people or animals who might threaten them.

The roofs have not survived but only one house had a window, so that if you had been living inside between 3100 and 2500 BC, any light would probably have come from the central fire.

Inside the houses there are a number of things we can recognize. On the left-hand side is a dresser with shelves, and cupboards are tucked into the walls. On the far side is a box bed.

On the floor there is a central hearth for cooking. Beside this there are flat stones for grinding and pounding flour and other foods, and set into the floor are watertight containers, perhaps for keeping water or live fish and shellfish.

huge enclosures made by cutting massive ditches into the soil and creating great walls of earth, or ramparts.

At Windmill Hill in Wiltshire archaeologists have found the site of a vast enclosure on top of a natural hill. The ramparts were dug out of ditches which enclosed an area of just under ten hectares. They have found other similar sites but do not know their purpose. Some have contained remains of houses but they may also have been used to enclose animals or hold markets. Such a complicated construction, built by hand with only (by our standards) simple tools shows that the people who planned and built it must have been very well organised.

Windmill Hill, in Wiltshire.

Making new tools

Farmers needed new skills and different tools to grow crops and herd animals. They still made tools and weapons from flint and stone, and they also made many objects out of wood, bone, leather and reeds (for baskets, for example) but hardly any of these have survived. What was new was pottery. For the first time in Britain, people started to make and use pottery. They dug the clay, then shaped and fired it to make pots which they used for storage and cooking.

The first farmers needed good quality stone for the large number of tools which they used, particularly for axes to clear the land. They needed something better than the poor quality of flint which lies on the ground's surface in many parts of Britain. The best kind of stone for these axes was hard, volcanic rock, which could be split into shapes. It was found in many places in England, Scotland, Wales and Ireland, but there was a great deal of it at Penmaenmawr in North Wales and at Great Langdale in the Lake District. The farmers took the stone which lay on the mountain slopes and used flint tools to work it into the right shape.

A flint mine in Norfolk

Farmers must have been on the look-out for large sources of stone, particularly good quality flint. In southern and eastern Britain they found it in seams of flint in the chalk below ground level. The first mines for flint were dug in Sussex before 3000 BC. The most famous, though, are at a place called Grimes Graves in Norfolk. The name of these flint mines is very odd. We think that Anglo-Saxon people (see page 50) probably gave this name to the place because the word for 'graves' in their language meant 'hollows' and the word Grimes comes from 'grim', meaning fierce.

From about 2100 BC the farmers at Grimes Graves discovered seams of very high quality flint. They dug deep, open pits and mined tunnels to take the flint out in large blocks. They dug out several hundred mines and then tipped the chalk and waste flint into the nearest worked-out pit. Each pit probably produced about eight tonnes of flint.

Working in the mines must have been hard. Using only their hands, flint tools and shovels made from the shoulder blades of oxen, the miners dug away the soft, sandy soil on the surface. They shifted the chalk and flint with picks made from the antlers cast off by red deer, wedges of bone and flint hammer stones. They used the flint they mined for all sorts of tools such as axes, arrow and spearheads, knives and scrapers for cleaning the skins of animals.

The miners were experts at their trade, but probably did not work there all the time. They stopped using the mines altogether around 1600 BC. By that time people all over Britain and Ireland had learned how to make tools from metal.

A cross-section of what the flint mine at Grimes Graves may have looked like. It had about 360 shafts and quarries. Although several of the mine shafts have been excavated, we can only guess at the sort of ladder system these mines used, because wood does not survive in these conditions underground.

Communication and trade

There is plenty of evidence in the prehistory of Britain to show that people communicated and traded over quite long distances. Stone axes made in Ireland have been found in Scotland, others made in Great Langdale have been discovered as far south as Wiltshire, and stone tools made in North Wales have ended up on the south coast of Britain. Flint blocks from the mines were carried to western and northern Britain. Some axes have even been found in Britain which are known to have come from Brittany, in France, and Scandinavia.

Society changed fast during the first farming period. In order to clear the land and build the settlements, to mine the materials for the tools which they then made, to herd, breed and train the animals and change the whole landscape of Britain, the people must have been highly organised. These ancient ancestors of ours continued to grow in number, and left other more mysterious and extraordinary monuments on the landscape.

People and goods travelled long distances, by boat on the sea and on rivers, and on trackways along high ground. In Somerset, a whole system of wooden trackways has been found. The most famous is known today as the Sweet Track (after Ray Sweet, the local man who discovered it).

It was built in about 3800 BC and so far about two kilometres of it have been uncovered. It was built of oak planks held in place by pegs made of alder and hazel. The Sweet Track was probably built by local people, so that they could make full use of the higher ground for farming and of the lower wetlands for hunting and fishing.

CHAPTER 3

A ritual landscape

❖

To us the words 'ritual' and 'religion' may mean a visit to a special building, such as a church, a synagogue, a mosque or a temple. Today it is almost impossible for us to guess at what may have been the beliefs of people who have left no written record of what they thought.

The lives of prehistoric people depended on the countryside around them. Hunters needed good supplies of food to kill or gather. Farmers

and their animals relied on the weather to ensure that supplies of crops would survive. Did they believe in an after-life? Did they believe that performing particular customs or rituals would bring good hunting or better weather? We do not know. Hunters probably held special ceremonies for their dead. Perhaps the famous paintings in caves in France and Spain were supposed to encourage successful hunts. We do know that later prehistoric peoples thought that 'spirits' lived all around them and influenced their lives.

In order to understand the beliefs of prehistoric people we must look for evidence. That usually means investigating buildings or structures which do not seem to have been used for living in. In the same way we can see from

This small chalk goddess was found on a pedestal in Grimes Graves. She was made at some time around 2000 BC and is probably a fertility figure, intended to ensure a good *supply of flint. The figure is also very similar to some found in Europe which can be linked to the worship of the goddess of the earth.*

West Kennet Long Barrow, Wiltshire, seen from the air. This 'house for the dead' must have taken a long time to build. It is a mound of earth about three metres high at one end and about 100 metres long. Ditches on each side provided the soil for the mound.

Before the mound was built, five chambers were constructed, leading off a straight corridor.

The barrow is well preserved, but the ditches along each side are missing. They have gradually filled up over the years, mainly because earth has slipped down from the mound. You can see that the entrance to the burial chambers has been blocked off by huge stones.

the shape of a church or mosque today that they are not ordinary buildings. Inside they contain special objects. They seem to be laid out for a kind of gathering or ceremony.

Monuments for the dead

We know that the first farmers built special monuments for their dead. These monuments not only cover up the remains of the dead but also mark the place of the burial in a spectacular way. The most common form of monument over the dead was a mound, today often called a barrow. These mounds were constructed in different shapes and sizes at different periods and the material the people used for building them depended on what was available locally.

Many of the monuments were made of stone. These stone-chambered burial monuments and other types of stone monuments from this period have been described as 'megalithic' from the Greek word, meaning 'big stone'. Some of the stones were massive. Building them must have required great effort, involving the whole community.

At West Kennet Long Barrow in Wiltshire archaeologists uncovered the remains of about fifty people who had been buried over a thousand year period beginning in about 3500 BC. Buried beside the dead bodies were objects such as pottery, beads and flint arrowheads. In many tombs the archaeologists have found ordinary, household rubbish. Was this part of a ritual too? We do not know.

Studying the bones of the people buried in West Kennet proved very interesting. Men and women were slightly shorter than people today, but they would have looked just like us. However, many children died very young and many adults would not have lived beyond the age of thirty. Practically everyone buried in West Kennet who was over the age of twenty-five had arthritis.

Some of the bodies buried in the tomb had been deliberately laid out. Earlier remains of the dead had been moved to one side to make room for them. Some of the dead were probably left outside, to rot before burial. We know that this was part of the burial custom at other sites, as it still is among some peoples today. The entrance to West Kennet, as in many other tombs, was blocked by huge stones which formed part of a 'courtyard' in front of the mound. Again, remains in other tombs show that this was probably the place where 'rituals' and ceremonies were held when the person died. There is evidence that they dug pits and lit fires, but what actually happened is still a mystery.

In about 3200 BC a group of people (archaeologists have estimated that there were probably about 400 of them) built an enormous burial mound at Newgrange, County Meath in Ireland, using 200,000 tonnes of turf and stones. It probably took them about thirty years. They built three burial chambers, in a cross-shape, at the end of a long, stone tunnel. They made the roof of the chamber by overlapping flat stones – a technique called 'corbelling'.

The builders of Newgrange not only put an enormous amount of effort into its construction, they also gave much thought to the way it was laid out. They carefully placed the entrance tunnel so that, at daybreak on Midwinter's Day (21 December), the sun shone through a space above the blocked door to the entrance. It lit up the chamber deep inside the mound. It must have been an amazing sight. To create this extraordinary monument the builders of the tomb were more than good planners and builders; they must have studied and worked out the movements of the sun and moon to calculate the exact position so that the sun shone through the door at that precise time.

Some of the most extraordinary burial monuments lie along the River Boyne in the east of Ireland. The most spectacular is at Newgrange because the mound has been partly reconstructed to give an idea of its huge size and how it looked. This is a view looking towards its entrance.

Inside Newgrange there are many examples of designs cut into the stones. The spirals here on the left were made by pounding or 'pecking' the surface of the stone.

Other tombs have different decoration, such as rectangles, triangles or lozenge shapes. These designs must have had some meaning for the people who used the burial mound, perhaps as part of what they believed in or the rituals they used in ceremonies, but whatever it was is lost to us today.

STONEHENGE

The stone circles at Stonehenge in Wiltshire probably form the most famous prehistoric ceremonial site of all. Even today enough of the circles survive to build up a picture of what it was once like. The first ceremonial construction was a henge built in 2950 BC. A bank and ditch enclosed a large circle, and two stones were placed upright to mark the entrance. About thirty metres from this entrance a much larger stone, now called the Heel Stone, was put up.

About 300 years later, the first stone circle was built inside the henge. Eighty-two stones were placed in two rings, one inside the other (called concentric circles). The most amazing thing is that these stones were probably brought to Wiltshire all the way from the Preseli Mountains in South Wales. It must have been an enormous effort to drag, and carry on rafts, stones weighing as much as four tonnes each.

The circle we see today was built in about 2300 BC. The builders brought nearly eighty stones about thirty

Stonehenge seen from the air. The snow on the ground makes some of the features of this monument stand out clearly. The trackway across the front of the stones is modern, showing where visitors have walked, and is now being repaired! The bank and ditch and the two mounds show up clearly.

Sarsen hammerstones found at Stonehenge were used to shape the stones and as packing around the base of the uprights.

kilometres to form a special circle of uprights with large capping stones. These local stones, called sarsen stones, also formed five separate 'arches' which are called trilithons (Greek for 'three stones').

Even at its earliest period archaeologists think that Stonehenge was used to observe the movements of the sun and the moon. Just inside the henge circle over fifty pits were dug. Some contained pieces of flint or red clay which might have been offerings. Later some of these holes were used to hold the cremated remains of people. It is clear that Stonehenge was an extremely important religious site, perhaps the most important in Britain.

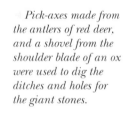

Pick-axes made from the antlers of red deer, and a shovel from the shoulder blade of an ox were used to dig the ditches and holes for the giant stones.

This close-up view of one of the trilithons shows what a feat it was to build this monument. These are sarsen stones brought from about thirty kilometres away, on the Marlborough Downs.

The stones must have been moved on rollers or sledges. Bringing them would have been hard work. The heaviest stone weighs about fifty tonnes and would have taken at least 500 people just to move it.

In this view you can see the Heel Stone through one of the arches. At the summer solstice, the longest day of summer, the sun rises and shines over this stone into the centre of the monument.

This stone circle is at Castlerigg in Cumbria. With thirty-three of the original thirty-eight stones still standing, it is one of the finest surviving circles in Britain.

Stone circles

There are more than 900 stone circles in Britain and there are also impressive groups in Ireland. But we are not certain what they were used for. They may have been built as ceremonial or religious monuments, but some experts think that some of them were designed for observing the planets and stars. Stonehenge is a good example of this. The early farmers had no calendar as we know it today. By placing the stones very carefully, perhaps after a year of observation of the skies, they could create a system for monitoring the seasons. They might watch the rays of the sun or moonlight fall over a certain stone and know exactly what time of year it was from its position. These calculations would tell them when seasons, and the ceremonies which went with them, were approaching.

Excavations at many stone circles have revealed pieces of human bone and broken pottery, suggesting that some sort of ritual had taken place. These and the remains of burning leave unanswered many questions about the beliefs of prehistoric people. A way of observing the seasons, a way of marking a death or for something else? We do not know. These monuments keep their secrets. Although the remains in them may add to our knowledge of how these ancient people lived and died, what they believed about life and death remains unknown. Occasionally, we may catch a glimpse, but that is all.

CHAPTER 4

Celtic Britain

❖

Soon after 1000 BC the climate in Britain began to change. This did not happen quickly, but slowly the average temperature fell by 2 °C. It became much windier and the amount of rainfall increased. These changes in climate affected the land, so that some of the farming peoples of Britain had to move to other places. Since about 1500 BC the population in Britain had been increasing and there were now farms and settlements in all areas. As the climate changed, some low lying coastal regions were gradually covered by the sea. Heathlands, which had always been quite difficult to farm, were abandoned. On the higher lands in Dartmoor and Wales sodden remains of plants began to rot to form a black, wet layer of peat which covered the soil. This bog could not be farmed. Even in fertile areas such as the midlands of Britain, people sometimes gave up their small fields and instead made large 'ranch-style' holdings, divided by great boundary banks and ditches.

Hundreds of people lived and worked inside the hilltop town of Maiden Castle, in Dorset. This is what archaeologists think the whole town looked like.

The houses were large and round, built of wood, with thatched roofs. You can also see the innermost defensive bank, with a strong timber fence on top. This was called a palisade and was made out of hundreds of wooden stakes.

Defending territory

Perhaps it was this decrease in the amount of good farming land, and large increase in the population, which brought about a change in society in Britain. The people created defended settlements, both large and small. Remains show that from about 1000 BC they preferred to build settlements on the tops of hills, which were easier to defend than ones in valleys. These settlements developed into 'hillforts', as they are called today.

There were probably about 3000 of these hilltop towns in Britain. The people who lived in them needed a strong defence against enemy tribes, as well as wild animals. First they chose a hill which had its own defences, such as steep sides. Then they built huge banks of earth

around the whole hilltop by digging out deep ditches. Sometimes they built steep stone walls in front of these banks.

Some hillforts, such as Maiden Castle in Dorset, are surrounded by several banks and ditches, built over the centuries as the inhabitants improved and modernized their defences. It must have taken a great deal of time, and hard work, to build such massive constructions.

Entrances to places which are defended are very important. The inhabitants need to come and go, and yet the forts must be strong enough to keep out an enemy. The hillfort builders thought up a clever type of entrance which made the enemy twist and turn between the high walls to look for the way in. It was like a small maze. Inside the entrance 'tunnels', the defenders could attack the invaders.

These hillfort towns were laid out in an orderly way. There were areas for the round or rectangular houses and areas set aside for workshops where craftworkers made objects such as iron or bronze tools. There were places for storing food, usually in the form of grain for grinding into flour during the winter and for replanting the following spring. These grain stores were often sealed holes in the ground. The hillforts were also trading centres where markets and fairs could be held.

Hillforts were not the only defended places on the landscape. Although the people lived inside these strong defences, the land they farmed was outside. They might bring their animals into the hillfort for protection, or perhaps keep them in specially built pens. They were often surrounded by smaller forts and defended villages and farms. One farm, found at Springfield Lyons in Essex, was encircled by a great ditch, while inside it were a rampart, or bank, a wooden walkway and defended gates.

In the wetter areas of England, Scotland and Ireland, people built defended settlements on islands in lakes, called crannogs. People in the north and west of Scotland built a different type of defended settlement, called a broch. Brochs were massive stone-built towers which tapered into a narrow point towards the top. The tower could be as high as fifteen metres. The 500 brochs found in Scotland are all similar. Archaeologists think there may even have been travelling groups of professional engineers who supervised those who built them. The massively thick walls of the tower contain staircases to the upper levels, and there is only one entrance. They were definitely built to keep people out.

At Craggaunowen, in County Clare in Ireland, a crannog has been reconstructed. A crannog was made of stones, rubbish and timber which were thrown into a lake to create an artificial island that formed the crannog. The water, as well as the strong wooden palisade, protected the people who lived in the round houses.

This is the broch at Clickhimin in Scotland. It had a stone wall with a walk-way which surrounded other buildings. These included round houses, a blockhouse to guard the only entrance, and the broch tower itself.

A decorated bronze scabbard for a sword found in County Antrim in Ireland. Celtic people fought with swords and spears and protected themselves with shields. They also used slings to hurl round stones very accurately at the enemy. A good sling-thrower could easily kill an enemy at a range of sixty metres.

Warrior peoples?

We have written evidence and objects from the people who lived in these unsettled times in Britain and Ireland. Archaeologists have found the remains of weapons and armour, such as swords, spears, shields and helmets. We know warriors rode horses and used lightweight chariots for battle. They probably raided each other's territory for cattle. Perhaps the remains found at Tormarton in Avon are evidence of just that. The bones of two young men were found buried in a ditch. One had a spear thrust through his pelvis; the other was wounded in the same place but also had a spear in his back and had had a blow on the head. This violent fight happened in about 1000 BC.

The written evidence comes from Greek and Roman writers who describe a people known as the Celts. The Celts lived in western Europe from about 700 BC. From about the fifth century BC writers in Greece began to describe attacks by peoples they called the *Keltoi*. The Romans called them *Celtae*. The different Celtic peoples seem to have spoken dialects of a similar language, which meant that they could understand each other. While some Celts were attacking Greece and Rome, others came over from Europe to Britain and Ireland. Some probably settled, others may have raided the coasts. They probably passed on ideas, and their language, to the people already living in Britain.

There is almost no evidence to show that the Celts could write, so all the written evidence comes from the point of view of the Greeks and Romans who, for most of the time, were their enemies. They emphasise the warlike character of the Celts and paint a picture of a fearsome people,

This is an excavated burial place of a young woman at Wetwang Slack on Humberside. Under her are the remains of the pieces of a chariot or cart. Only the iron fittings and the horse-bit survive – the wood has rotted away. To accompany her on her journey to the next world are a variety of objects: a side of pork, a dress pin, a mirror and a bronze box.

terrifying to behold. They tell us that the Celts were very excitable and that the warriors in Celtic society were tall, fair-haired and fierce. One writer, a Greek called Strabo, said that they were 'mad keen on war, full of spirit and quick to begin a fight'. To frighten their enemies in battle, the warriors would comb their hair with lime to make it stand on end like the quills of a porcupine. Stripped to the waist, they rushed shouting into battle. Some of them added to the clamour by blowing through a tall animal-headed trumpet, called a carnyx. Celtic men liked to decorate their bodies, sometimes with tattoos or by painting patterns with a blue dye made from a plant called woad.

One Roman account tells how in one battle the Celts used 4000 chariots. Each chariot would have had two horses. Another account describes how terrifying such an attack must have been. The sight and the noise would have been deafening as the chariots thundered over the ground:

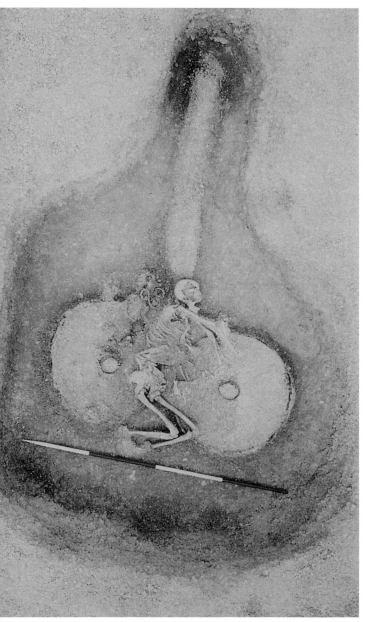

> In chariot fighting the Britons [Celts] begin by driving all over the field hurling javelins, and generally the terror inspired by the horses and the noise of the wheels are sufficient to throw their opponents' ranks into disorder. Then, after making their way between the squadrons of their own cavalry, they jump down from the chariots and engage on foot.

Living in tribes

The Celts were not just warriors. They were an organised people who had their own laws and were ruled by nobles who were kings, princes or chiefs of their own tribes or clans. We know the names of some of the leaders and their families. We know that women had a special place in Celtic society – some fought as warriors and could be leaders of their tribe. Skilled storytellers, called bards, had an honoured place in society as well. Famous events in the life of the Celts would be told and retold in stories passed from one bard to another. Craftworkers with special skills were also highly regarded, particularly those who worked with metal, making all the weapons and armour for the nobility (see page 34).

As well as living in defended hillforts, Celtic people also lived on individual farms and in small villages of perhaps five or six families. They created small fields which could be ploughed in one day. Like the early farmers (see page 16) they used the ard, a simple plough pulled by two oxen. They grew two main cereal crops – wheat and barley. Both were grown for bread, and barley was also used to make beer. They grew vegetables, such as small beans (which we call Celtic beans), and other plants we now think of as growing wild, such as vetch. They grew the flax plant so that they could make linen cloth from its stalks; they fed its leaves to the animals and made oil from its seeds.

They kept a variety of animals – cows, horses, goats, pigs, sheep and possibly chickens. We know that the Celts also had dogs, which they may have used for hunting wild boar. We know too that they kept slaves. Most were probably prisoners taken in war and were counted as the property of the owner, just like any other possessions such as tools or houses.

Thick cloaks and twisted gold

From written accounts and remains it is possible to build up quite a detailed picture of what these Celtic people looked like. Both men and women wore their hair long, although sometimes women would plait theirs. The Greek historian, Diodorus Siculus, described how some men wore beards and how long flowing moustaches were popular:

> Some shave off the beard, while others cultivate a short beard; the nobles shave the cheeks but let the moustache grow freely so that it covers the mouth … when they are eating, the moustache becomes mixed with the food and when they are drinking, the drink passes through it, as it were, like a sort of strainer.

In the middle of the twentieth century a farmer, ploughing a field at Snettisham in Norfolk, came across a collection or 'hoard' of metal objects. There were at least sixty-one gold and silver 'neck ornaments' or torcs, two bracelets, and 158 coins, as well as rings and other fragments of tin and gold. This is part of the hoard.

Celtic clothes were colourful and bright. The craftworkers would dye the yarn before weaving their cloth. We know that they used natural ingredients to make the colours – for brown they used the bark of the birch tree, black came from the bark of the elder tree, red and orange from the root of goose-grass, blue from wild berries and yellow from the young shoots, flowers and bark of gorse. Diodorus Siculus said that the Celts 'wear striking clothing, tunics dyed and embroidered in many colours, and trousers which they call *bracae*. They wear striped cloaks, fastened with a brooch.'

A description of the Celtic Queen Boudica tells us more about how a noble-woman looked: 'She wore her great mass of hair the colour of a lion's mane right down to her hips. She always wore a richly coloured tunic, a thick cloak fastened with a brooch and a large necklace of twisted gold around her neck.'

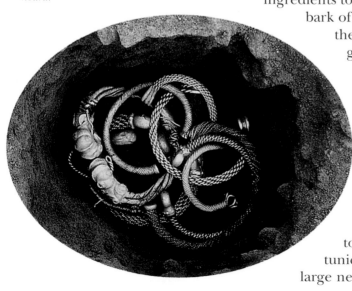

CELTIC METALWORK

Iron ore was first mined in Britain about three thousand years ago. Archaeologists think that some of the earliest workings were at Brooklands in Surrey. The tools used by a blacksmith for working the iron were much the same as those used by blacksmiths until quite recently: tongs, hammer, anvil and poker. They also worked with bronze and gold – silver came from abroad and the few silver objects which have been found were probably brought from Europe.

Objects found on archaeological sites or by accident (on building sites for example, or on farmland) show that the Celts liked to decorate the things which they made to use and wear; it seems that the more valuable the object the more care they took to decorate it. They needed special tools to make patterns in the metal. Their decoration used strange patterns of coils, circles and lines; no one knows whether they had any meaning.

Archaeologists describe Celtic patterns as 'abstract' art, because where they do seem to represent animals or humans they use only the outlines to create the decoration.

Today, the objects illustrated here are some of the greatest treasures in the British Museum in London. Two thousand years ago, in the first century BC, they were made and used by the Celts for show, for war, or for using every day.

Greek and Roman writers noticed how proud the Celts were of their appearance. We know they liked mirrors because many have been found in graves.

This is the back of a bronze Celtic mirror found in Desborough in Northamptonshire. It would have been highly polished on the other side. The decoration has been carefully worked out with short lines. A sharply-pointed tool would have been used to scratch the design on to the surface of the metal.

This is the horned helmet of a Celtic warrior. This helmet was found in the river Thames near Waterloo Bridge. It may have been lost in battle or thrown in as an offering to the gods.

Gold seems to have been a valuable metal even in those times; it seems to have been used particularly for making neck rings or 'torcs'. This torc is made of a mixture of gold and silver and was found at Snettisham in Norfolk. Although other torcs have been found, this is probably the most beautiful.

This Celtic shield probably belonged to someone important – a nobleman perhaps. The bronze face of the shield was discovered in the river Thames at Battersea in London. It was probably attached to a wooden base, which has rotted away. The red decoration was made from enamel. This was coloured glass which was heated and then shaped into small pieces to fix on to the metal.

This is the handle of a bucket which was found in a grave at Aylesford in Kent in 1886. It was made by wrapping decorated bronze sheets around a wooden container. The bucket may have been used for some ordinary purpose, but in the grave it held the burnt or cremated remains of the skeleton.

Priests and gods

The Celtic people were very religious. They believed that gods and spirits were around them all the time and could be dangerous. They had to be worshipped and offerings had to be made to them. Water was particularly important to the Celts, perhaps because the lack of it could make such a difference to their way of life; a bad harvest could be disastrous. Springs, wells and pools were therefore often sacred, and many metal objects were thrown into them as offerings to the gods.

We also know that there were Celtic priests, called Druids. They were an educated class in society who were particularly troublesome to the Romans when they arrived in Britain (see page 39). The Irish saga, *Táin*, tells us that women could be Druidesses. We know from other evidence that the more important, older women in the household were often thought of as being able to prophesy (or foretell) future events, such as the outcome of a battle.

Much of the evidence for the Celts comes from other parts of Europe. This silver cauldron from Denmark, which might have been used for sacrifices or a water-offering, shows a detail of a god holding two figures.

The Celts believed that the oak was a sacred tree and the Druids would look for shady oak-tree groves for religious ceremonies. At certain times of year they would cut down mistletoe from high up in the trees to use in rituals. For this they used blades called sickles, made of gold.

The Celts also sacrificed animals and people to their gods. The Roman and Greek writers described their ceremonies with a fascinated horror. The Roman historian Tacitus, writing later, in the first century AD, tells how the Druids in worshipping their gods would 'drench their altars in the blood of prisoners and consult their gods by means of human entrails'. Another Roman writer described their victims:

> They believe that the gods prefer it if the people executed have been caught in the act of theft or armed robbery or some other crime, but when the supply of victims runs out, they even go to the extent of sacrificing innocent men.

This strange Celtic stone, called 'the Turoe Stone', is decorated with abstract Celtic designs. It was found in Ireland, and was probably used in rituals, but no one knows its exact purpose or meaning.

One famous example from Britain is Lindow Man, also known as Pete Marsh, a name given to him by archaeologists! In 1984 machines digging for peat at Lindow Moss in Cheshire uncovered a body. Archaeologists were soon on the scene to carry out proper excavations. The body was that of a man who probably lived in about the first century AD. He was so well preserved in the peat bog that archaeologists could reconstruct a model of him from what they found: he had a beard and a moustache, he was wearing a fox-fur band on his left arm, his last meal was wholemeal bread made of wheat and barley, but mixed in with other plants – cow parsley, heather, fat hen and dock; his fingernails were carefully trimmed, (no one with such finger nails could have worked with his hands or fought, so perhaps he was important); he had probably drunk some kind of potion which contained mistletoe.

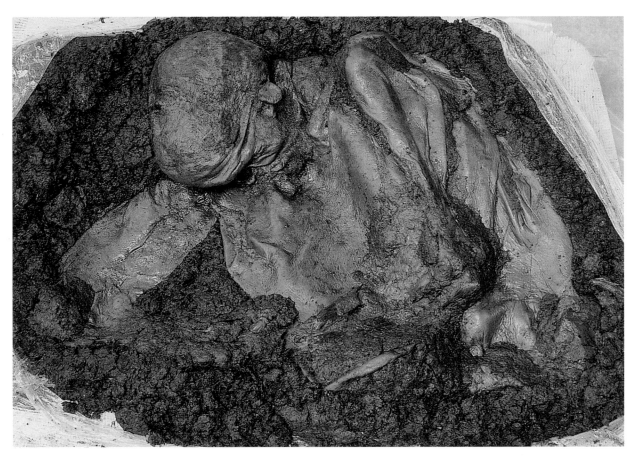

These are the well-preserved remains of Lindow Man after he had been examined and conserved in a laboratory.

Archaeologists have been able to make this reconstruction model of his head because he was so well preserved.

How did this man meet his death? He was definitely killed, and it seems to have been no ordinary killing. He was knocked unconscious with an axe and struck in the back. This broke one of his ribs. He was then strangled with a cord which broke his neck. When he was dead, his throat was cut and he was dropped, face down, into a pool in the peat bog. Why did he suffer such a violent death? Was he a human sacrifice? We cannot be certain, but it is probably the best guess.

Exchanging goods

We know that there was a good deal of general contact and trade between the peoples of Britain and parts of Europe in the first century BC. The Greek writer Siculus told how the Celts who lived in the south-west of Britain were particularly welcoming to strangers and had adopted 'a civilized manner of life' because of their contacts with merchants and other peoples. He describes how the merchants from Europe bought tin from the Celts. Objects of fired clay and metal were also being exchanged between Britain, Ireland and parts of Europe among people speaking a similar language.

As trade increased, some settlements on the coast grew and developed into ports. One which has been studied in detail is on the

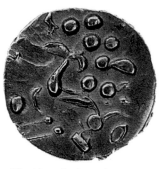

The idea of using coins probably began among peoples in Europe and was copied by people in Britain. This gold coin was minted in Kent in the first century BC. The design (like many other coins of the period) shows the shape of a horse.

south coast of England at Hengistbury Head in Dorset. The site, near Christchurch Harbour, had been occupied by earlier hunting and farming peoples. In the first century BC it became a major international port. Tin, silver, copper and pottery arrived here from the west country, lead and pottery from further inland and wine, coins and pottery from France.

During the first century BC the Romans extended the frontiers of their empire as far as Gaul (now mainly France). Some refugees from the Roman occupation came across to Britain, but there was also a chance for goods, especially luxury goods, to be imported from the Roman world. These are often found in the graves of wealthy members of Celtic society.

Tribes and chieftains

More than a million people must have been living in Britain by the first century AD. The written evidence tells us the names of the tribes and of some of the people, especially chieftains and queens. Some of the large hillforts, such as Maiden Castle, were probably the strongholds of the chieftains of the tribes. In the south-east of Britain, however, a new type of settlement was created. The Roman Latin term used to describe them was *oppidum*, which really means 'a fortified town'. Long stretches of banks and ditches were built to cut off and defend large flat areas. These were areas of settlement, places for industry and places from which powerful chieftains could control river crossings. It was to one of these towns, Camulodunum (now Colchester, in Essex) that the Roman Emperor Claudius marched in AD 43. The prehistoric period of the history of Britain and Ireland was coming to an end.

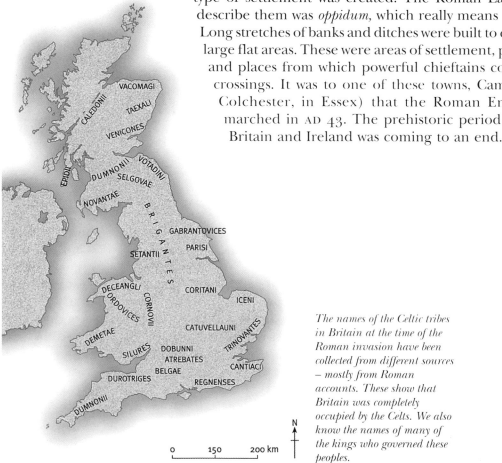

The names of the Celtic tribes in Britain at the time of the Roman invasion have been collected from different sources – mostly from Roman accounts. These show that Britain was completely occupied by the Celts. We also know the names of many of the kings who governed these peoples.

CHAPTER 5

The Roman province

❖

In the first century BC the huge Roman Empire first began to make contact with the island of 'far away Britain', as one Roman poet called it. At first this contact was through trade with the rich Celtic nobility in places like Camulodunum (Colchester). The merchants from the empire brought luxury goods, such as gold, small bronze statues, wine and pottery from Gaul, Spain and Italy. However, peoples who lived on the edge of the empire could expect to receive more attention from the Romans than just visits from merchants.

In 58 BC Julius Caesar, who was governor of Rome's most northerly province in Italy, wanted to make the north-western frontier of the Roman state safe, and to bring honour to himself. The frontier stretched as far as Gaul, a part of Europe which then covered roughly the same area as modern France, southern Holland, Belgium, Switzerland and part of Germany. Caesar set out to conquer the Celtic tribes of Gaul. He was so successful that the Roman politician Cicero said that, 'Before … we only had a route through Gaul … Caesar has fought very successfully against the fiercest of peoples in great battles and made them part of the Roman state.'

As part of this campaign Caesar turned to the Celtic tribes in Britain. He thought they were helping the Gauls, and he wanted to see if it was worth launching a full-scale invasion.

This shows the head of one of the most famous of Roman generals. Julius Caesar led the Roman army in campaigns in Gaul and in the invasion of Britain. He wrote his own account of his campaigns, and much of what we know about Roman Britain comes from this.

Caesar's invasions

Julius Caesar invaded Britain twice. The first time, in 55 BC, he landed somewhere near Deal in Kent with about 12,000 troops. The Romans dreaded the sea crossing to Britain. Caesar himself wrote that they were faced with grave difficulties:

> The size of the ships made it impossible to run them aground except in fairly deep water; and soldiers, unfamiliar with the ground, with their hands full, and weighed down by the heavy burden of their arms, had at the same time to jump down from the ships, get a footing in the waves, and fight the enemy … [who were] boldly hurling javelins and galloping their horses … these perils frightened our soldiers, who were quite unaccustomed to battles of this kind …

In the first invasion Caesar forced the chieftains of the tribes in what is now Kent (see the map on page 38) to accept the authority of Rome. In the following year, 54 BC, he invaded again with about 37,000 troops. This time he marched inland as far as Hertfordshire and defeated the powerful Catuvellauni tribe. The Trinovantes in Essex surrendered.

These two invasions showed that Rome was powerful and prepared to use force to extend and protect its empire. The southern tribes of Britain had surrendered, but the conquest was not completed. Caesar left no troops to occupy the country because he needed his army in Gaul. However, trade and contact continued and more people in southern Britain became used to Roman ways – although at a distance.

'Barbarians beyond the sea'

When the Romans decided to add new territory to their empire they asked themselves two main questions: 'do we have enough troops?' and 'will we recover the cost of the invasion and will the new province "pay its way"?'

In AD 43 the Emperor Claudius asked those questions and decided a full-scale invasion and occupation of Britain was possible. Claudius, who unlike some other emperors was not a military man, also wanted honour and fame for himself. He collected information about Britain from up-to-date reports and studied Caesar's own accounts. One description by Tacitus, the Roman historian, shows why the

These are the two faces of a coin made in the reign of the Emperor Claudius to celebrate his victory over the Britons, which was written in Latin on the coin - DE BRITANN. His name is abbreviated on the right of his picture: CLAVD (V=U). Claudius is shown on the reverse of the coin, riding on horseback on the top of a triumphal arch.

Romans thought Britain was worth invading: Britain, he wrote, had 'gold, silver and other metals to make it worth conquering.'

Claudius did not lead the invasion force of 40,000 men himself but joined his commander-in-chief, Aulus Plautius, when the army had successfully fought its way to what is now London. Claudius then arrived from Gaul, bringing some war elephants, to make a real impression on the native people. He marched with his army to Camulodunum (Colchester) in Essex, which was then the capital of southern Britain. In Rome there is still a triumphal arch built by Claudius which records his capture of the Celtic stronghold: it tells how he received the submission of ten kings and one queen. For the first time, it says, 'the Barbarians beyond the sea' were under the power of the Roman people.

Richborough, on the coast of Kent, was the landing place of the army of the Emperor Claudius. In AD 43 the sea was close to the site which you can see here, but it did not look like this then as it was built over and developed right through the Roman period. The Romans built the stone wall later, to defend the coast of Roman Britain against attacks from Europe (see page 18).

Claudius stayed only sixteen days in Britain, but his army went on to establish Roman rule in the south and south-west of the country. In the rest of Britain the Romans did not find the people easy to conquer. In a number of campaigns their armies pushed out from the south-east of the country and by AD 47 had established a frontier stretching from Devon to the river Humber. In the next ten years the Romans campaigned in Wales, occupied Cornwall and moved the frontier north to the borders of what is now Scotland. Permanent military forts were established in Wales, but the tribes there remained difficult to subdue. The Romans fought many campaigns in Scotland and occupied some parts, especially on the east coast, but eventually they were forced to withdraw and established frontier walls, Hadrian's Wall and the Antonine Wall.

In the AD 70s an invasion of Ireland was proposed but never carried out. Although the Romans never invaded Ireland, some Scotti, a people from there, settled in the north and west of Britain and then others took back to Ireland a variety of Roman goods and ways; Latin words which began to be part of the vocabulary, clothes which were Roman in style and even a new religion – Christianity.

When Hadrian visited Britain – probably in AD 121 or 122 – he toured the province and ordered his soldiers to build a huge stone wall across its northern limits, to protect the inhabitants from invasion and attack. The wall, known as Hadrian's Wall, ran for 117 kilometres from Wallsend on the River Tyne to Bowness on the Solway Firth.

Guard-posts were built at regular intervals along the wall. In between them were look-out towers. The soldiers were stationed in forts along or behind the wall.

(below) Boudica, queen of the Iceni, in a bronze statue in London, put up in the early 1900s. The chariot has scythes on the wheels, which it would never have had. Boudica was certainly fierce. One Roman writer described her as 'a very big woman, terrifying to look at, with a fierce look on her face' and a harsh voice.

There were setbacks for the occupying Romans. The most serious was the revolt in AD 60 when tribes in eastern Britain massacred the inhabitants of several towns and one Roman army legion of nearly 6000 soldiers. The uprising was led by Boudica, the queen of the Iceni tribe who, with her daughters, had been brutally attacked and humiliated by the Romans. Many of the tribes in the south joined her, and at first her forces were successful, as they burned and killed the inhabitants first of Colchester and then at the new port of Londinium. Greatly alarmed, the Romans gathered an army and met Boudica somewhere in

the Midlands. The slaughter was terrible. It was said that 80,000 Britons died and 70,000 on the Roman side, including those Britons who supported them. The Britons were defeated and it is said that Boudica poisoned herself.

Ruling Britannia

Now that Britannia, as the Romans called it, was a new province of the Roman Empire they could gradually introduce their own Roman laws. The Romans wanted each province in the empire to be controlled as part of the whole, so that it was a safe place for everyone to live and work in.

Most of the people of Roman Britain were already living on the island when the Romans arrived. Tens of thousands of soldiers increased their numbers. There were also Roman officials and merchants.

The soldiers of the Roman army lived in camps. Some of these were large permanent fortresses built for whole legions, such as those needed to control the invasion and occupation of Wales at Caerleon (in the south), Wroxeter (in the midlands) and Chester (in the north). When the Roman authorities were satisfied that the people they had conquered in an area were living peacefully the army pulled out, leaving only police forces and patrols at key places.

This is the tombstone of a Roman centurion called Favonius. His full name is written, in abbreviated form in Latin, on the top line of the inscription. The inscription also tells us that he was in the Twentieth Legion. The tombstone was found, in Colchester, Essex, with the face damaged – probably by Boudica's forces.

The army's first task was to build roads. Good roads made it easier for them to move quickly to conquer rebellious tribes. Then the officials would follow. The emperor would appoint a governor, to rule on his behalf. He would serve for three to five years; he would be commander-in-chief of the Roman forces in the province, chief administrator and chief judge. He would be responsible for seeing that Roman law was obeyed and have a large staff to carry out his orders. In addition, the emperor would appoint another official called a procurator to work for him. His job was to collect taxes, look after the estates and the valuable mines, and see that the gold, silver, iron and lead were exported back to Rome.

Living as Romans

The biggest change caused by the Romans in Britain was the number of towns which they developed all over the province. In pre-Roman Britain (see page 29) the power of Celtic tribal chieftains and the nobility covered a large area which usually included some defended towns. These new Roman towns not only looked completely different; they were organised in a different way. There were different types, each built for a different purpose.

Some were called *coloniae*. These were colonies of ex-soldiers who settled down with a plot of land and some money. The Romans could rely on these Roman citizens to rule sensibly through the town council, and gradually build a proper Roman town. Colchester, the province's first capital, was an example of a *colonia*. Other towns were *municipia*. These were towns where the local people had been given a charter to run their own affairs. Verulamium (now St Albans) was an example of a *municipium*. The third type of town was called a *civitas*. *Civitas* is the Latin origin of our word for citizen; it meant someone who lived in a town or city; to the Romans this was a 'civilized' place. These towns were established as the main centre for a tribal area. They organized some of their own affairs but the governor had the final say, at least at first. Wroxeter was an example of a *civitas* (see page 45).

What was a Roman town like? We know that a town or city today means a large settlement of people with places for living, working, shopping and entertainment. In Roman times that was also true, but a visitor to a town in Roman Britain would expect to see a number of particular buildings and places, including a planned road system which linked the town with others and the countryside around. On the edge of town, there would be cemeteries for the disposal of the dead. The town itself would have a wall with gates (if the people had permission from the emperor), a laid-out street pattern with buildings in regular blocks, a water supply with fountains and water basins in the street, and a proper underground sewage system.

The public buildings would be grouped around an open central space such as a square called the forum. Here there would be a public

The main towns and roads in Roman Britain in the second century.

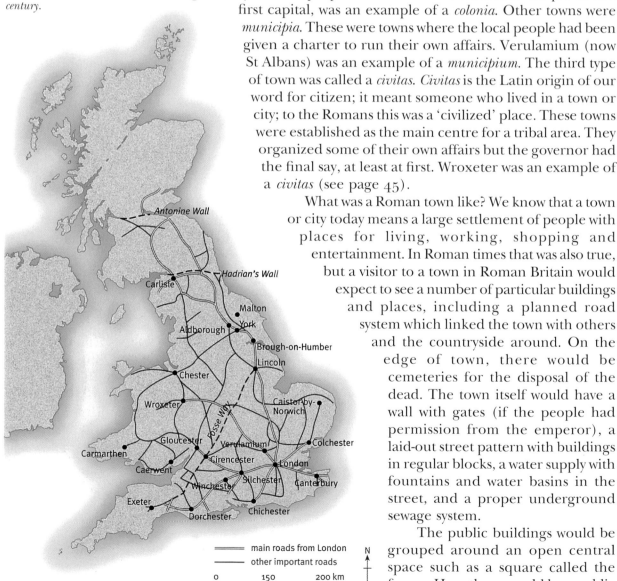

Antonine Wall
Hadrian's Wall
Carlisle
Malton
York
Aldborough
Brough-on-Humber
Lincoln
Chester
Caistor-by-Norwich
Wroxeter
Fosse Way
Gloucester
Verulamium
Colchester
Carmarthen
Cirencester
London
Caerwent
Silchester
Canterbury
Winchester
Exeter
Chichester
Dorchester

═══ main roads from London
——— other important roads

0   150   200 km

N

This drawing shows what the whole of the city of Wroxeter might have looked like. It was built on a flat plain overlooking the River Severn. The land drops sharply away to the river and provides a good defence on that side.

All around the city ran a large bank and ditch with a wooden wall on top. The main road through Britain, later called Watling Street, ran through the centre of the city. It began at Richborough in Kent (see page 45) and ended in Wales.

Part of Wroxeter Roman city survives above ground, or has been excavated and conserved on the surface.

hall for meetings, law courts, council offices, baths, markets and temples. There would also be main shopping streets with workshops and small factories, as well as places for leisure and entertainment such as a theatre, perhaps even an amphitheatre. Much of the work in these places would be done by the slaves which the Romans took from the British tribes.

Houses might be heated with hypocausts, a type of underfloor central heating. There would certainly be painted walls and ceilings and at least some mosaic floors. The food gradually became more like Roman food as various herbs and spices were brought from other parts of the empire. The Romans were particularly fond of the strong fish sauce called *liquamen*.

The Romans forced the people of Britain to live by their system of government and way of life, but they also wanted to persuade them to live as Romans. Tacitus describes how the Roman aim was to make a life of peace and quiet seem attractive to the tribes of Britain, so that they would prefer that to fighting. They 'encouraged the building of temples, public squares and good houses'.

The Romans introduced schools, and with them a new language – Latin. Not everyone learned it, of course, but it was necessary if you wanted to do well in Roman Britannia. Tacitus mentions that they 'educated the sons of the chiefs ... the result was that instead of loathing the Latin language they became encouraged to speak it'. This gave an

In gladiatorial combat men were forced to fight to the death for the crowd's amusement. In Britain evidence comes from amphitheatres and objects like this decorated pot. It was found in Colchester and illustrates scenes from the gladiatorial shows. Pictured here is Memnon (on the left), a heavy armed gladiator called a secutor.

opportunity, to boys, to take up a job with the Romans, which might mean leaving their own province and travelling to other parts of the empire.

By the time the Emperor Hadrian came on an official visit to Britannia in AD 122 many people had settled into a regular Roman way of life. Some had even begun to dress as Romans: Tacitus records that, 'our national dress came into favour and the toga was everywhere to be seen'. Contact with travellers – merchants, craftworkers and officials – kept the people of this far away Roman province in touch with what was happening in the rest of the empire. In towns they could enjoy themselves at the baths or the theatre, or go to see the spectacle of the gladiatorial games in the amphitheatre.

Before the Romans came the Celts had many farms. Caesar wrote that ' the population is exceedingly large, the ground thickly studded with homesteads … and the cattle very numerous'. Celtic farmers were efficient enough to feed a large population, but the way the Romans farmed would have seemed extraordinary to the Celts. As the Romans drove their roads and tracks through the countryside, cleared and drained land and even built canals in some places, the changes in the appearance of the landscape must have been astonishing. The Romans also created large farming estates (some of them owned by the emperor), made the mines bigger and used slaves for work in them and on the land.

The main building at the Roman villa at Lullingstone in Kent has been completely excavated. Here you can see the remains of low walls preserved under a protective building. In the foreground are the rooms of the villa's private bath block.

Roman buildings in the countryside were different too. They called a farm a *villa*. The word was used to include the house of the farmer and the family as well as the buildings for the slaves, animals and produce. These places would have seemed huge beside the much smaller Celtic farms surrounding them. By the first century AD a Celtic farmer would probably want to build a new 'Roman' house and farm buildings.

The Romans brought their own religion and religious ceremonies with them when they invaded Britain. The Romans worshipped all sorts of different gods and goddesses from different parts of their huge empire. The people in Britain could worship Roman gods, although many of the Celtic gods and goddesses were worshipped still beside Roman ones. For example, in Bath there was a temple to Sulis Minerva who was a combination of the Celtic goddess Sulis and the Roman goddess Minerva. A popular god, especially for soldiers and merchants, was Mithras who was originally worshipped in Persia. His secret and mysterious religion was introduced into Britain and temples have been found at, for example,

Evidence for Christian worship in Britannia comes also from the discovery of objects used in church services. This extraordinary find of silver objects was made in the small Roman town of Durobrivae (now Water Newton in Cambridgeshire). They were probably made in the early fourth century for a wealthy Christian family, who gave them to a Christian community in the town.

London (the capital city) and the forts of Segontium (in Wales) and Housesteads (on Hadrian's Wall).

Christianity had become an important religion in parts of the Roman Empire, even though it was banned in the early period. Britons probably were unaware of Christianity until the later part of the second century AD. After that we do know of churches being built at, for example, Richborough in Kent and at the town of Silchester in Hampshire. Private churches in villas have also been found. The most famous is probably the one at Lullingstone Villa where in the mid-fourth century AD top-floor rooms were made into a chapel with Christian wall-paintings (now in the British Museum). It was in the fourth century AD that Christianity became the official religion of Rome and people could then worship freely in churches.

Attacks from all sides

Throughout the history of the empire the Romans had to deal with uprisings and attacks from beyond its borders. By the third century AD there was serious unrest in many parts of the empire. In the 250s there were uprisings in the German provinces and from AD 260 to 274 three emperors took power for themselves and ruled the west of the empire, from Hadrian's Wall to the Straits of Gibraltar and the Alps, in opposition to Rome. Raids on the coasts of Britain and Gaul meant that strong forts had to be built as a defence, and town walls were also repaired and strengthened. In the fourth century AD the Picts from Scotland, the Scots from Northern Ireland, the Attacoti from the western isles and the Franks and Saxons from Europe threatened Britain. In AD 367 a huge number swept south across Hadrian's Wall and besieged York.

The fourth century also saw another serious threat to Roman control of Britain. In AD 350 a Gaul called Magentius declared himself Emperor of Rome in opposition to the true Emperor Constans. Many people in Britain went to fight for him in Europe. He lost against Constans and Rome did not restore the army in Britain to its full strength. Other emperors took troops to fight on the continent – in AD 383 and 407.

By the beginning of the fifth century AD most of the Roman army in Britain had gone. For those British people who now lived as Romans there was no organised army to defend their way of life. In AD 410 the Britons sent a petition to the Emperor Honorius asking for help. He replied that they must from now on 'see to their own defences'. A final appeal to Rome was made in AD 446. The British monk Gildas, writing much later, tells of a letter sent to Rome that year, pleading for help:

> The barbarians are driving us into the sea and the sea is driving us back to the barbarians. Two forms of death wait for us, to be slaughtered or drowned.

No help came.

The end of Roman control

The end? People have often supposed that Roman Britain came to an abrupt end in the fifth century AD. But a Roman way of life had existed in Britain for nearly 400 years. It did not just disappear overnight. There may have been no central control, but many aspects of Roman life must have remained for some time. We know that the city centre at Wroxeter had been rebuilt in the Roman style in the late fourth century, perhaps by a local chieftain from Ireland or Wales.

Roman Britain did come to an end, of course, but only gradually. In the future, ways of life were to change again, as fresh waves of invaders and settlers came to Britain.

CHAPTER 6

The coming of the English

❖

Snapped roof trees, towers fallen,
the work of the Giants, the stone-smiths
mouldereth …

Came days of pestilence, on all sides men fell dead,
death fetched off the flower of the people;
Where they stood to fight, waste places
and on the acropolis [temple] ruins.

This bleak picture of ruin, death and destruction, darkness and plague is a description, probably of Bath, written about three hundred years after the Roman period in Britain. The Roman ruins, which could still be seen, it said were 'the work of Giants'. The carefully ordered world of the towns and villas of the Romans had fallen into decay. Britain broke up into small kingdoms led by warlords.

In the centuries after the Romans left Britain, their forts, like this one at Hardknott in Cumbria, fell into ruins.

This period used to be called the 'Dark Ages' by historians, partly because there was so little written evidence to tell us about it. Much of our evidence comes from the work of archaeologists. It can tell us a good

deal about the way people lived, even if we can put few names, if any, to the people themselves. We also know enough to realise that in the period from 450 to 800 lie the beginnings of answers to such questions as 'why are there different countries in the islands of Britain and Ireland?', 'why is English the language most of us speak today?' and 'why do some people speak Welsh and others Gaelic?'

Pevensey Castle, Sussex. The outer walls of this castle were built by the Romans in the middle of the fourth century. It was one of many forts which the Romans built to defend their province against raiders from across the sea.

The new invaders

Before the end of the fourth century Britain's coasts were already being attacked from the sea by new invaders. These were the Irish and the Picts in the west and north, and the Saxons and other peoples, together known as Anglo-Saxons, who came from Europe. At first the Roman army fought them off but by 410 the army had gone. A few Anglo-Saxons were already living in Britain, mostly as soldiers. According to the British monk, Gildas, the British invited some of them to Britain, paying them to fight against the northern invaders from beyond Hadrian's Wall. But enemies come in different forms. In 446 plague ravaged the country. Many died and the Anglo-Saxon newcomers, moving further inland from the south and east coasts, saw their chance and turned their weapons against their weakened British allies.

'Anglo-Saxon' is a name used now to describe several different peoples. The Angles, Saxons and Jutes came from northern Germany and Scandinavia. Frisians and Franks came from lands which are now part of France, Holland and part of Germany. The English we speak today has its roots in the Anglo-Saxon language and by the eighth century, three hundred years after the first Anglo-Saxon invasions, the word 'Englisc' was being used to describe the people in southern Britain.

Gradually these new settlers drove the British warlords west, to the hills, where they perhaps used some of the old Celtic hillforts to defend themselves. Certainly excavations show that some were rebuilt around this time, but there is not enough evidence to say who might have used them. By the beginning of the sixth century the Angles, Saxons and Jutes had settled widely in Britain. A British lament described how the Northumbrian English laid waste Shropshire in the seventh century:

More common was blood on the field's face
Than ploughing of fallow

The power of legend – who was Arthur?

The Anglo-Saxon advance was not always victorious. Certainly, later writers tell of a huge battle at Mount Badon, which the British won. Later scraps of written evidence suggest that there was a British war leader, called Arthur, who may have fought for more than one British war band, and held back the enemy's advance at the end of the fifth century.

By 600 the fame of this leader was known to the Welsh poet who spoke of one warrior who had 'glutted the black ravens' on the wall of the stronghold, 'even though he was no Arthur'. Long afterwards an account written between 960 and 980 described 'the battle of Badon in which Arthur bore the cross of our Lord Jesus Christ on his shoulders for three days and nights and the Britons were the victors'. No one is sure where the battle took place.

A later chronicle tells of Arthur's birth on the rocky Cornish coast at Tintagel Castle – but by then his story had become full of magical events. Arthur is perhaps the most mysterious figure in history; his name occurs in the myths of Wales, Britain and Europe, yet there is almost nothing to show that he ever existed.

The making of kingdoms

By the early seventh century the Anglo-Saxons were ruling most of Britain, but not its most westerly corners (Wales and Cornwall) or the north (see the map on page 52). Only in those regions did the British manage to keep their independent kingdoms. In the west by 550 there were Welsh kingdoms of Gwynedd, Dyfed, Powys and Gwent. In the north the Picts were the largest group. Tribes from Ireland created the kingdom of Dalriada on the west coast, and the main British kingdom was Strathclyde.

Not all the British people fled before the Anglo-Saxon advance. Many would have stayed and, as the years passed, as they had done with the Romans before, intermarried with the invaders, creating mixed settlements, living side by side. Some Anglo-Saxon kings had British names, and they may have divided land in the same way as the Celtic ancestors of the British.

The Anglo-Saxons settled in small groups. The 'cynn' (the kin or tribe) was a community of the lord and his followers and the lord, the 'cyning' (king) was the guardian of the kin. To the Anglo-Saxon warrior, to be part of a war band led by a strong leader was a matter of life and death; loyalty between king and follower kept the group together.

The hub of the settlement was the hall. Anglo-Saxon poets speak of the warmth of the smoke-filled hall. Outside lay a dangerous world of moor and sea, hunger and wild animals – and other enemy tribes. A man without a lord and companions had little protection and much to fear.

The poets spoke of a king as a 'battle-winner', a 'plunder-lord', a 'bracelet-giver'. His warriors would fight for him, and consider it shameful to withdraw from battle and survive his death. In return they expected their reward in treasure, land, cattle and slaves. Some of the names of these leaders survive today; Hastings in Kent was the home of the Haestingas, the followers of Haesta; Reading in Berkshire was the home of the Readingas, the followers of Reada.

Between 500 and 700 some of the leaders of the smaller kingdoms conquered their neighbours. By the late 700s 'bloodshed and sword' had created a number of larger kingdoms. Lesser kingdoms paid tribute money to these stronger kings. Sometimes one king would become more powerful than all the others. Later writers called them 'Over-ruler' or 'Britain-ruler'. The changes which were to end in England becoming a single kingdom had begun.

DUMNONIA Celtic and British kingdoms
ESSEX Anglo-Saxon kingdoms
– – – – – – Offa's Dyke

The Anglo-Saxons gradually pushed the Britons westwards:

conquests by 600

conquests by 800

0   100   200 km

Anglo-Saxon settlement between 600 and 800. Gradually, the Anglo-Saxons pushed the Britons westwards, creating a number of larger kingdoms by the late 700s.

Everyday life

Day-to-day living was as much about survival as warfare. Finds from excavations of village sites have revealed many details about early Anglo-Saxon daily life. One, now called West Stow in Suffolk, has been almost completely excavated. The lands along the river Lark had been farmed for thousands of years before the Anglo-Saxons chose this place to settle.

Only three of four families lived in the small village of Stowa. Each one had two sorts of buildings, both made of wood with thatched roofs. One, which is long and called a hall by the archaeologists, had a hearth in the centre. The other type of family building they call a sunken house. These are wooden tent-like buildings which had a dug-out area below the floor. Sometimes people may have lived in these, but usually they were workshops or stores.

The people of Stowa were farmers, who kept cattle, sheep, pigs, geese and chickens. They grew wheat, rye, barley, oats and peas in the fields around the houses and added to their diet by hunting deer and wild fowl, and catching fish. They would grow all their own food, eating mostly bread or porridge with meat for special occasions and brewing beer from barley. They might have been able to trade grain if there was a surplus, but they would certainly have exchanged animal hides and clothes for other luxury items. At Stowa they made iron objects (such as knives), pins and combs of bone, and pottery.

Some of what we know about Anglo-Saxon people comes from remains found in their graves. Death for Anglo-Saxons who were not Christian meant setting out on a journey. They would be buried with things which they would need and were most valuable to them. Finds from burial sites show that people were often buried in fine clothes, with their treasured possessions. A sword was a very valuable possession and might be handed down from father to son; for most men their weapon would be a spear. People might also be buried with everyday objects such as bone combs, knives, or spindle-whorls for weaving. Sometimes very small fragments of cloth survive in the graves, perhaps attached to the back of a brooch as one of the burials at West Heslerton in North Yorkshire showed.

These objects tell us something about the clothes people wore, and how they made them. Women often wore long flowing gowns fastened at the shoulders with big brooches, and they might decorate the cuffs with stitching, and hang a purse from a belt around the waist. They would

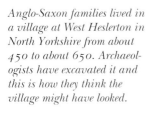
Anglo-Saxon families lived in a village at West Heslerton in North Yorkshire from about 450 to about 650. Archaeologists have excavated it and this is how they think the village might have looked.

wear jewellery of all kinds – rings, necklaces, pins and bracelets. Men usually wore short tunics over leggings with leather laced boots. In cold weather cloaks fastened with large brooches would keep them warm.

By 750, trade was becoming an important part of daily life. Growing trading settlements were called 'wics'. On the south and east coasts people gathered to live in these larger settlements, trading with people from Europe. The largest was Hamwic (now Southampton). Remains of streets show that they would have been crowded with houses and workshops, and the finds have included objects from all over Europe. Inland, trading posts grew where the important roads crossed. The kings and chieftains controlled this trade and sometimes made these trading settlements their headquarters. London had such a settlement (now partly covered by Trafalgar Square). York, called Eoforwic was another. Some smaller trading settlements were on the lower reaches of rivers, such as Fordwich in Kent and Ipswich in East Anglia.

As villages and towns grew, written documents show that the kingdoms of Anglo-Saxon England became well-ordered places with agreed rules. People expected their leaders to judge those who broke the rules. There were written codes, for example, which showed the lists of fines which a leader could impose.

This is the first page of Beowulf. *The manuscript was written on parchment, and is now kept in the British Library.*

An Anglo-Saxon hero

The poems and stories of the Anglo-Saxons were composed to be sung or spoken aloud to feasting warriors in the king's hall. Only long afterwards were they written down. The poets tell of heroes and their great deeds; of lords who provided shelter and food in their halls, and their warriors who provided 'helmet' and 'shield' in war with courage and loyalty.

Perhaps the most famous 'heroic' poem is *Beowulf*, written down between the eighth and ninth centuries. The hero is Beowulf himself, a war-leader from Scandinavia who is a slayer of dragons. In one story he rescues the land of the Danes from the man-like monster Grendel. In the other he risks all for a treasure-hoard stolen from earls and guarded by a fire-breathing monster. The monster kills the hero and the poet speaks of the treasure-hoard of 'the thick gold and bracelets'. He describes the funeral-pyre, a fire made 'so high and broad that the seafarers might see it from afar'. The poet ends, telling how Beowulf's warriors mourned their king, not only praising his courage but,

> They said he was of all the world's kings
> the gentlest of men, and the most gracious,
> the kindest to his people, the keenest for fame.

A remarkable discovery

During the late summer of 1939, when the nations of Europe were about to be plunged into another world war, in a corner of England near the Suffolk coast, archaeologists were making a remarkable discovery. With war only days away, they had found the grave of an Anglo-Saxon leader which held some of the most beautiful objects ever discovered. The name of Sutton Hoo was about to enter the nation's history.

Working day and night, the archaeologists knew that the site could hold the key to questions which had remained a mystery for centuries. As they uncovered the treasure, the mythical world of Beowulf sprang to life, a world of splendour, wealth and power where such treasure was the highest prize.

The treasure itself had been part of a ship burial; no human remains were found but the richness of the objects, chosen for the journey to the next world, showed that this person must have been important. The objects included cloaks and leather shoes; weapons – spears, sword and axehammer; armour; a sceptre and

(above) One writer has called this 'the ghost of the Sutton Hoo ship'. Excavations in 1939 uncovered only the impressions of the timbers; the structure itself had rotted away.

(right) This helmet was found in the Sutton Hoo burial site. It is finely decorated with scenes of fighting and is made of iron with overlays of bronze, silver and gold.

This large gold buckle, shown here in its actual size of just over 13 centimetres long, was probably used on a belt to hold a sword. The 'interlace' – a criss-cross decoration – is often found on jewellery and in stone carving from the sixth and seventh centuries. If you look closely at the decoration you will see strange animals weaving in and out of the pattern and biting themselves. The Sutton Hoo treasure can be seen in the British Museum in London.

This is the metal lid of a purse which contained thirty-seven gold coins. It was fitted on to a belt and the purse itself was probably made of bone or ivory which has now rotted away. The metal is gold but there are inlays of garnet, stone and glass. Apart from the interlace, you can see men and animals and in the centre are two falcons swooping on two ducks.

an iron standard; jewellery, a purse and gold coins; buckets, cauldrons, bowls, dishes and spoons; a lyre (a small harp) with six strings; and drinking horns. The metalwork of some of the objects shows that they came from Europe.

This might have been the grave of Raewald, a king of East Anglia, who was rich and powerful. He probably died in about 625. Others think it might have belonged to Sigebert, an East Anglian king who lived slightly later. Whoever he was, he belonged to a new world in which kings had enormous wealth, power and contact beyond the shores of Britain.

Pagan kings become Christian

In 431 Pope Celestine sent Palladius as bishop 'to the Irish believing in Christ'. Palladius was followed by other missionaries, one of whom was Patrick, later to become St. Patrick. Patrick's life was certainly colourful and it is not surprising that he is the best remembered. What we know about him comes from his own writings. His father was a landowner and a Christian, and probably lived in the area around Carlisle. When he was about sixteen Patrick was captured by raiders, probably Scotti from Ireland who took him back with them to Ireland as a slave. After six years he escaped by ship to Brittany (part of Roman Gaul). He returned to his home district when he was about twenty-five years old. There he trained for the priesthood, and he returned to Ireland as a bishop sometime after 450. During the next hundred years or so, Patrick and the other missionaries who followed converted the Irish to Christianity.

In 597 Pope Gregory I in Rome decided it was time to persuade the Anglo-Saxon kings to give up their heathen beliefs and become Christian. The monk he chose to lead a group of about fifty missionaries was Augustine. King Aethelbert of Kent received the Christian missionaries from Rome kindly, gave them a dwelling in Canterbury, but did not at first wish to become a Christian himself. Gradually he changed his mind, letting the monks build a church in Canterbury. Augustine became its first archbishop. Anglo-Saxon England had entered a new era.

To the English kings, with their ever-increasing power and wealth, this new religion was attractive. European leaders were already Christian; now they would be on equal terms. There were other benefits. Christian priests could read and write. Anglo-Saxon kings could not. Who better to write their documents?

Not all Christians came from Rome. Some had already arrived in the north of Britain from Ireland and converted some of the northern kings. In 563 an Irish monk, called Columba, had founded his monastery on the island of Iona on the west coast of Scotland. When King Oswald of Northumbria asked for someone to convert the Northumbrians, Aidan and some followers came and settled on the island of Lindisfarne, where they built a monastery.

Although the 'Irish' and 'Roman' churches had links they did have some disagreements about how they organized themselves. They argued most fiercely over the date of Easter. Each tradition observed it on different dates. The bishops, becoming rather bad-tempered, put their case before the king of Northumbria at a special conference at Whitby in 664. The king decided in favour of the Roman date for Easter, much to the displeasure of the Irish bishop who returned home in a huff.

This chalice was found in Ardagh in County Limerick in Ireland in 1868 and is now in the National Museum of Ireland. The chalice would have been used for the giving of wine at the communion mass in church.

Made in the eighth century, this chalice is an example of the rich ornament used at the time. It is made of beaten and polished silver. The bowl and stem are decorated with engraving and gold, copper, enamel and amber, and malachite.

Preaching the word of God

It probably took more than seventy years for the English kings to give up their old gods and become Christian. However, converting kings and their courts to Christianity was not at all the same as converting the ordinary people. Where were they to go to hear the Christian message of the bishops and their priests? Monasteries and churches were the answer. Between 650 and 850 kings and their bishops built hundreds of monasteries.

These early monasteries were rather like settlements. Sometimes ruled by women, they included a variety of people as well as priests, nuns and monks. They were centres of religious life and became magnets for trade. Called *minsters,* they echo today in the names of towns such as Ilminster and Kidderminster.

The age of Bede

In the great eighth-century monasteries, Anglo-Saxon culture was enriched by imported European ideas, and they became international centres of learning and art. Their churches, often elaborately built in stone, mark the beginnings of English architecture. Wealth and security gave monks and nuns the chance to study. They copied the stories of the Bible, the psalms and the lives of the saints for others to read. These copies, called manuscripts (from Latin *manu scribere,* 'to write by hand') could take years to make and were beautifully decorated and illustrated:

One of the earliest bishops, Aidan (see page 57) asked the Northumbrian king for the island of Lindisfarne so that he could build a monastery there. It was a lonely place which Bede described like this: 'On the bishop's arrival the king gave him ... the island of Lindisfarne ... As the tide ebbs and flows, this place is surrounded twice daily by the waves of the sea like an island and twice, when the shore is left dry, it becomes again attached to the mainland.'

to make the manuscripts beautiful was to honour God. Perhaps for the first time, Britain was taking a dynamic part in the growth of European civilization.

In the monastery at Jarrow in Northumbria the greatest Anglo-Saxon scholar, Bede, wrote his *Ecclesiastical History of the English People*, which he finished in 731. His main purpose was to explain how the English became Christian, as the work of the various groups of monks and priests from Rome and Ireland gradually built up a unified Faith. But he also describes in vivid detail the Roman rulers of Britain, the arrival of the Anglo-Saxons, the wars in which they won territory from the Britons and Picts, and the growth of their kingdoms. Bede has been called 'the Father of English History'; he may even have been the person who first invented the phrase 'English people' to describe the various Anglo-Saxon groups.

Offa and the Mercian kingdom

It was nearly two centuries after Bede's death before the 'English people' were genuinely united. In the meantime kings were becoming steadily more powerful, ruling ever larger areas. In the seventh and eighth centuries the great Midland kingdom of Mercia, which had its centre in what is now Staffordshire and Derbyshire, was the richest and strongest kingdom, and often dominated weaker ones around it. The Mercian king, Offa, who ruled for nearly forty years from 758 to 796, was regarded by some as the king of all England south of the Humber. This claim is exaggerated, but Offa probably controlled greater resources than any ruler in Britain had done since the Romans left. By now more people could read and write, and better systems of administration were being developed to control trade and gather tax. Wealth and productivity were increasing, so that kings could become very rich.

In the 780s Offa decided that he had had enough of the Welsh tribes raiding on his borders. A later Welsh chronicle records that,

(above) The Lindisfarne Gospels were copied and decorated at the monastery on Lindisfarne in 698. Work on manuscripts like this is described as 'illuminated', because it looks as though it is lit from the inside. The letters and borders are painted in bright colours, sometimes with gold or silver leaf attached. Each of the four Gospels begins with a magnificently decorated page, such as this one.

It is interesting to compare the design with the Sutton Hoo treasure. Some of the patterns are very similar.

This coin shows King Offa's head and name. English kings had been issuing coins since the seventh century, but Offa's are the most beautiful to have been made in Britain since the Romans left. The picture shows him looking rather like a Roman emperor: was he starting to think of himself as a different kind of ruler?

Offa caused a dyke to be made between him and Wales … that is called 'glawd Offa' … and it extends from one sea to the other … from the south near Bristol to the north above Flint.

Offa summoned thousands of men, who dug a ditch up to 2.5 metres deep and up to 20 metres wide. The dyke cut through the land as railways and motorways do today, stranding farms and villages from once near neighbours. Over a thousand years later, some of the dyke still stands.

Despite all Offa's efforts to create a stable kingdom, Mercian power collapsed in the 820s. The future lay with the kings of the West Saxons, the people of Hampshire and Dorset who controlled the great port of Southampton and the mineral resources of the south-west.

All Offa's efforts proved in vain. His son's reign was as short as his was long. Ecgfrith died only months after his father. In East Anglia and Kent the subject-kings gathered in revolt. The new Mercian king, Cenwulf, won the first round. The captured Kentish leader was brought to Mercia in chains and mutilated. His eyes were put out and his hands cut off. Holding on to power was an ugly business, but the king was lucky to escape with his life.

The Dark Ages?

For the first two hundred years of Anglo-Saxon rule in Britain most of what we know comes from archaeological evidence from sites of burials, villages and towns. By the eighth century there is more written evidence – Bede's *History*, the charters and *Beowulf* are the most important. Even so, there is still very little; one historian has written that,

> what we know hangs by so narrow a thread that it is certain as certain can be that there was a great deal about Anglo-Saxon England about which we do not know and never will know anything.

We know enough, however, to realise that in the west and far north there were separate kingdoms of mainly British tribes. In the Anglo-Saxon kingdoms the rulers created laws and systems of justice which continued long after they had gone. The people traded and made things which were some of the most exquisite ever produced, founded monasteries and settlements which became centres of great art and learning. Towards the end of the eighth century however everything they had achieved was threatened. A new wave of invaders appeared from across the sea.

CHAPTER 7

The Vikings invade

❖

The year was 789. From across the sea three ships carrying Northmen landed on the coast of the kingdom of the West Saxons. The king sent a messenger to find out who they were, but he never returned. The account records that the Northmen slew the messenger. The next sentence foretold the threat to come: 'those were the first ships of Danish men which came to the land of the English'. In the ninth century many people were terrified of these Northmen, or Vikings. In England they called them 'wolves to be feared' and 'stinging hornets' and in Ireland 'ruthless, angry, foreign, purely pagan people'. The word Viking comes from *vikingr* which meant pirate or raider in the old language of the Norwegians.

In the eighth and ninth centuries all the people who lived in the Scandinavian countries of Norway, Sweden and Denmark were known as Vikings. In their own countries they were farmers, town builders and great traders. Their artists and craftworkers made beautiful objects. Many were travellers and sailors who sailed the seas looking for plunder, trade, and land for new settlements.

This Viking boat, nearly twenty-two metres long, was found at Oseberg in Norway. It has been reconstructed in the Viking Ship Museum near Oslo. A thousand years ago it was the burial ship (like the one at Sutton Hoo, see page 55) of a royal lady who died in the ninth century. It was probably originally used as personal transport for the royal family.

'Wolves from the sea'

This is part of a stone grave marker from the ninth century found on Lindisfarne island. It shows Viking raiders with axes and swords, probably attacking the church at Lindisfarne in 793.

The key to the success of the Vikings in their quest for plunder and trade was their ships. They were wonderful builders of ships and boats and made three types. For trading along their coasts and for fishing they built rowing boats. The most popular was a four-oared boat called a *faering*. For trade further away, especially between countries, they made wide ships called *knarrs*. To attack other lands the Vikings built narrow *longships*, which could hold up to 200 warriors and travel at great speed.

Whether they were farmers or merchants, all Viking men had to fight. In battle they wore padded leather tunics or, if they could afford them, mail coats. To protect their heads they had iron or leather helmets, which often had nose and eye protectors. Round shields made of wood kept off blows from the enemies' weapons and the Vikings themselves used a variety of weapons – swords, daggers, spears and axes.

In the eighth century the Vikings began to travel further away from their Scandinavian homelands. Some were searching for new land to farm. In about 700 Viking settlers landed on the Shetland Islands off the north of Scotland. By 860 there were Viking settlers in Iceland. We know that the Viking Eric the Red reached Greenland in 986. By about 1000 there were Viking settlements in north America, in Labrador and Newfoundland. Vikings from Sweden crossed the Baltic Sea and travelled into eastern Europe. In 860 Viking ships even reached Constantinople, and in 862 a Viking called Rurik founded Novgorod in Russia.

Many Vikings travelled not to settle but on raiding parties to capture gold, jewellery, animals, food and slaves. They began raiding the coasts of Europe in about 790. One description tells how, in 793, 'The ravaging of the heathens destroyed God's church at Lindisfarne, with much plunder and slaughter.' These 'heathens' were Viking raiders who had sailed from western Norway. To kill the monks and steal their treasure was not difficult. A scholar and teacher, called Alcuin, wrote to Aethelred, the king of Northumbria, in this same year:

> We and our fathers have now lived in this fair land for nearly three hundred and fifty years, and never before has such an atrocity been seen in Britain as we have now suffered at the hands of a pagan people.

The Vikings attacked again in 794. They raided the monastery at Jarrow the following year and sailed down the coast as far as Dorset. From 835, Vikings from Denmark were attacking East Anglia and the south coast of England. At about the same time Vikings, mainly from Norway, were raiding Ireland, even sailing their ships inland along rivers. In both Britain and Ireland the people built defences against the raiders, but by the 840s the Vikings had begun to build their own fortified camps, called *longphorts*, so that they could protect their ships and spend the winter on enemy territory.

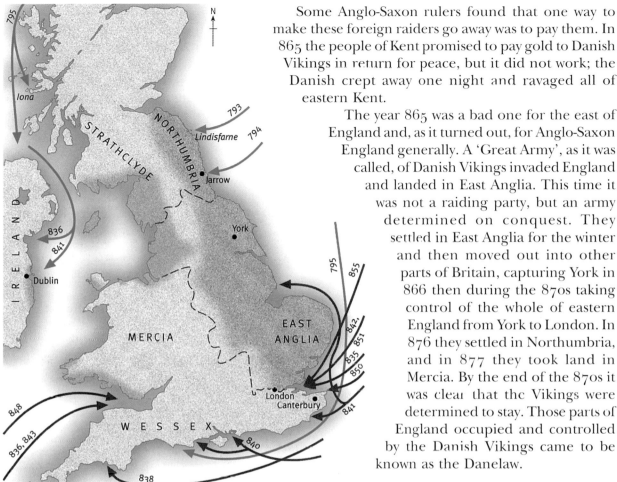

Some Anglo-Saxon rulers found that one way to make these foreign raiders go away was to pay them. In 865 the people of Kent promised to pay gold to Danish Vikings in return for peace, but it did not work; the Danish crept away one night and ravaged all of eastern Kent.

The year 865 was a bad one for the east of England and, as it turned out, for Anglo-Saxon England generally. A 'Great Army', as it was called, of Danish Vikings invaded England and landed in East Anglia. This time it was not a raiding party, but an army determined on conquest. They settled in East Anglia for the winter and then moved out into other parts of Britain, capturing York in 866 then during the 870s taking control of the whole of eastern England from York to London. In 876 they settled in Northumbria, and in 877 they took land in Mercia. By the end of the 870s it was clear that the Vikings were determined to stay. Those parts of England occupied and controlled by the Danish Vikings came to be known as the Danelaw.

Viking attacks from Norway
Viking attacks from Denmark
— — boundary of the Danelaw
0   100   200 km

The early Viking attacks from Norway and Denmark were made by raiding parties, but in 865 a Danish 'Great Army' settled in East Anglia for the winter.

(right) This Viking stirrup, with brass inlay, was found in the river Cherwell near Oxford. As soon as they landed the Vikings seized horses to take them inland. They moved fast along the old Roman roads, threatening the kingdoms of the Anglo-Saxons.

The Vikings in Ireland

In their search for plunder, Vikings, mainly from Norway, sailed round the Hebrides as far as Ireland. The first recorded raid took place in 795 when they attacked Iona and the Irish monasteries at Inishmurray and Inishbofin. Then larger fleets began to arrive. In 840 one account records that they spent the winter on Lough Neagh, plundering and attacking monasteries and settlements. They took 'bishops and superiors and scholars prisoner and killed others'. The next year they built a defended ship harbour on the mouth of the River Liffey. This encampment was the beginning of the Viking town of Dublin. The settlement was soon to become a great Viking city, trading with other European ports.

Later on the Vikings established themselves at Cork, Waterford, Limerick, Arklow, Wicklow and Wexford. The Irish kings fought back with growing success. In 902 they forced the Vikings to leave Dublin. They returned fifteen years later, but over sixty years afterwards, in 980, the Irish King Maelsechnaill decisively defeated the Vikings at the Battle of Tara and they were never again a real threat.

Viking settlement

Most of the written evidence we have about the Vikings in England comes from a Christian account called the *Anglo-Saxon Chronicle* which was written much later, in about 892. The Vikings were the enemy and the *Chronicle* paints a picture of warriors intent on slaughter and destruction. Remains found at places where they settled give another side of the picture – of a people who were farmers and traders, skilled at making decorated objects to use and wear.

Most Vikings were farmers and lived in country settlements. The *Anglo-Saxon Chronicle* records that the Viking leader, called Halfdan,

This Anglo-Saxon manuscript drawing of a Viking ship shows what a terrifying sight to the inhabitants they must have been as they sailed towards the coasts and up rivers, full of warriors preparing to land and attack.

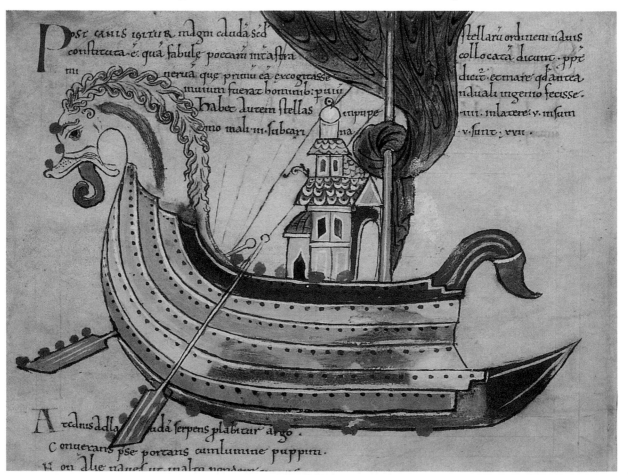

'shared out the land of the Northumbrians, and they proceeded to plough the land and make a living for themselves'. Some villages were taken over by the new Viking settlers, others were newly built. Wherever they settled they built the same sort of farm. They grew a variety of crops such as wheat, oats, barley and vegetables (cabbages, beans and carrots). They kept animals such as cattle, sheep, pigs, goats, geese and chickens but they also hunted animals, birds and fish for extra food. They were also great traders and liked to exchange their goods in town markets. The town of Jorvik gives us a wonderful idea of Viking town life (see page 66).

During the ninth century, Vikings from Norway began to settle in the islands off the north coast of mainland Scotland. They moved into the islands of Shetland and the Orkneys. From there they went to the Hebrides, the west coast of Scotland, the Isle of Man and Ireland. At that time there were four different peoples living in Scotland. The Picts lived mainly in the far north, English lived south of the Firth of Forth, while there were Britons and Scots on the west coast (see page 51). In the north it was the Picts who were forced to give way to the Viking settlers.

The Picts left no written documents but their carvings give us a glimpse of how they lived. This Pictish carved slab shows a battle scene, probably of a battle with the Angles, with some of the warriors on horseback.

Remains from one of these Viking settlements at Jarlshof on the island of Shetland show how large a farm or farmstead could be. There was a farmhouse and outbuildings for cattle and storage. There was a blacksmith's shed, and probably a bath house where water would be thrown over heated-up stones to make a sauna. The main building was the farmhouse. It was long, with only one room, which had a kitchen at one end and places for sleeping and eating at the other. Over the next four hundred years Jarlshof grew into a small village on the water's edge, and fishing became very important to its inhabitants.

The foundations of Norse houses at Jarlshof, on Shetland.

The Vikings who lived at Jarlshof and elsewhere would have worn brightly coloured clothes. Women often wore scarves on their heads, an ankle-length dress of wool or linen, with an overdress held on by great brooches. Men wore woollen trousers with a shirt or tunic on top. Both women and men wore jewellery as decoration, such as brooches, finger or arm rings and necklaces.

JORVIK

By 875 the town of York in England, which was then called Eoferwic, already had a long history. It was once a Roman fortress and city and then the Anglo-Saxon capital of Northumbria. When the Vikings attacked it on 1 November 866 it was already a busy trading centre. The Vikings massacred many of the town's inhabitants, but then left an Anglo-Saxon called Egbert to rule in their name. They returned for good in 875 and the town, called by the Viking name Jorvik, developed into the Viking capital of Northumbria. It stands on the river Ouse, which allowed ships easily to reach the centre from the North Sea. This was essential for Viking trade. Viking Jorvik was a large bustling place, full of noise and smells! As the town grew it became an important centre for trade and crafts. One writer described it as 'filled with treasures of merchants from many lands'.

Remains uncovered in Jorvik have revealed a great deal about the way of life there. The houses and other

Making glass beads would have been one of the many industries in Jorvik. The beads were mostly strung on necklaces but some of the smaller ones were probably sewn on to clothing as decoration.

The houses at Jorvik were built inside long strips of land running back from streets and divided from neighbouring plots by fences of wooden wattlework.

The preservation of wooden material was so good on the 'dig' that both wattle walls and timbers of the Viking houses were uncovered. Some of them are still preserved in their original position in the Jorvik Viking Centre below street level.

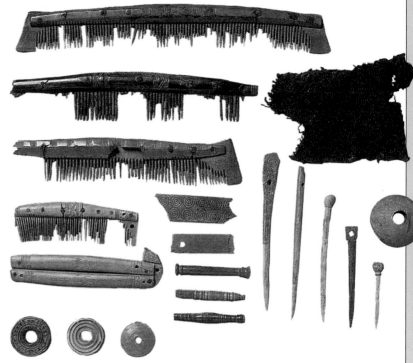

We know the Vikings liked to play games with counters. One game was called 'hnefatafl' for two players. The Viking playing counters are made of chalk and antler. The board is modern.

Leather-working was important for clothes, shoes, belts and dagger sheaths. This is a well-preserved leather shoe. The bone underneath is an ice-skate, highly polished on one side.

buildings nearby which have been excavated were in a street called Coppergate. The word *gata* is a Danish Viking word for 'street'. The word 'copper' is taken from the cupmakers (*koppr* means cup) who had their workshops and businesses there. Coins were struck and all sorts of objects and utensils were made from iron, gold, silver, pewter and bronze; kilns provided pottery kitchen utensils and lamps.

The remains of the houses show us how ordinary people lived. They were quite small, measuring about 7 by 4.4 metres. There were usually no walls inside so the family slept, sat and ate in the one space with an open fire in the centre of the room. People could sit on benches built on to the side walls of the house. Each one probably had a table and maybe a chest to store clothing, bedding and valuables. At the back of the houses were work-shops, yards, wells, storage and rubbish pits as well as cesspits.

These are some of the very unusual remains from Jorvik which tell us something about how the Vikings dressed. Even pieces of woollen cloth have been found, including Viking socks!

The 10,000 people who lived in Jorvik would have needed combs for their hair – to make it look good and to get rid of the fleas (also found by archaeologists!). They carved bone and antler to make such things as combs, hairpins, needles and counters.

Names as evidence

During the tenth and eleventh centuries many ordinary Vikings would have gone on living and working on their farms and in towns. The names of places they built often echo the Anglo-Saxon name: the modern name of York, for example, came from Anglo-Saxon 'Eoforwic' meaning 'wild boar settlement'. This changed to the Viking *Jorvik* meaning 'wild boar creek'.

Place names which today end in '-*by*' were originally Viking, meaning a settlement of any kind, either town, village or farm. The ending '-thorpe' was also often used for a small settlement. The endings '-with' and '-thwaite' described settlements made by clearing woodland. Some place names in Scotland end in '-wick' which comes from the Viking word *vik* meaning a bay or an inlet.

The Vikings settled long enough in Britain and Ireland to create lasting settlements. But their conquest, which had begun in 865, was not to go unchallenged. In the south of Britain in 870 King Aethelred and his brother Alfred were planning their defence, as the Danish Vikings were preparing to invade their kingdom of Wessex.

THE ENGLISH ROYAL LINE OF SUCCESSION

❖

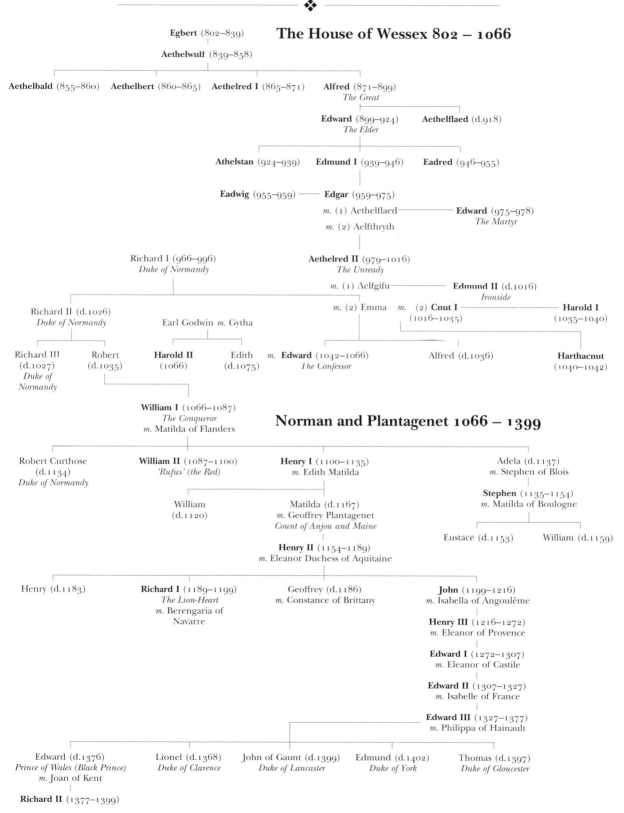

The House of Wessex 802 – 1066

Egbert (802–839)

Aethelwulf (839–858)

Aethelbald (855–860)   Aethelbert (860–865)   Aethelred I (865–871)   Alfred (871–899)
The Great

Edward (899–924)   Aethelflaed (d.918)
The Elder

Athelstan (924–939)   Edmund I (939–946)   Eadred (946–955)

Eadwig (955–959) —— Edgar (959–975)

m. (1) Aethelflaed ———— Edward (975–978)
The Martyr

m. (2) Aelfthryth

Richard I (966–996)   Aethelred II (979–1016)
Duke of Normandy   *The Unready*

m. (1) Aelfgifu ———— Edmund II (d.1016)
Ironside

Richard II (d.1026)   *m.* (2) Emma   *m.* (2) Cnut I   Harold I
Duke of Normandy   Earl Godwin *m.* Gytha   (1016–1035)   (1035–1040)

Richard III   Robert   Harold II   Edith   *m.* Edward (1042–1066)   Alfred (d.1036)   Harthacnut
(d.1027)   (d.1035)   (1066)   (d.1075)   *The Confessor*   (1040–1042)
Duke of
Normandy

William I (1066–1087)
The Conqueror   ## Norman and Plantagenet 1066 – 1399
m. Matilda of Flanders

Robert Curthose   William II (1087–1100)   Henry I (1100–1135)   Adela (d.1137)
(d.1134)   'Rufus' (the Red)   *m.* Edith Matilda   *m.* Stephen of Blois
Duke of Normandy

William   Matilda (d.1167)   Stephen (1135–1154)
(d.1120)   *m.* Geoffrey Plantagenet   *m.* Matilda of Boulogne
Count of Anjou and Maine

Eustace (d.1153)   William (d.1159)

Henry II (1154–1189)
m. Eleanor Duchess of Aquitaine

Henry (d.1183)   Richard I (1189–1199)   Geoffrey (d.1186)   John (1199–1216)
The Lion-Heart   *m.* Constance of Brittany   *m.* Isabella of Angoulême
m. Berengaria of
Navarre

Henry III (1216–1272)
m. Eleanor of Provence

Edward I (1272–1307)
m. Eleanor of Castile

Edward II (1307–1327)
m. Isabelle of France

Edward III (1327–1377)
m. Philippa of Hainault

Edward (d.1376)   Lionel (d.1368)   John of Gaunt (d.1399)   Edmund (d.1402)   Thomas (d.1397)
Prince of Wales (Black Prince)   *Duke of Clarence*   *Duke of Lancaster*   *Duke of York*   *Duke of Gloucester*
m. Joan of Kent

Richard II (1377–1399)

Lancaster and York 1399 – 1485

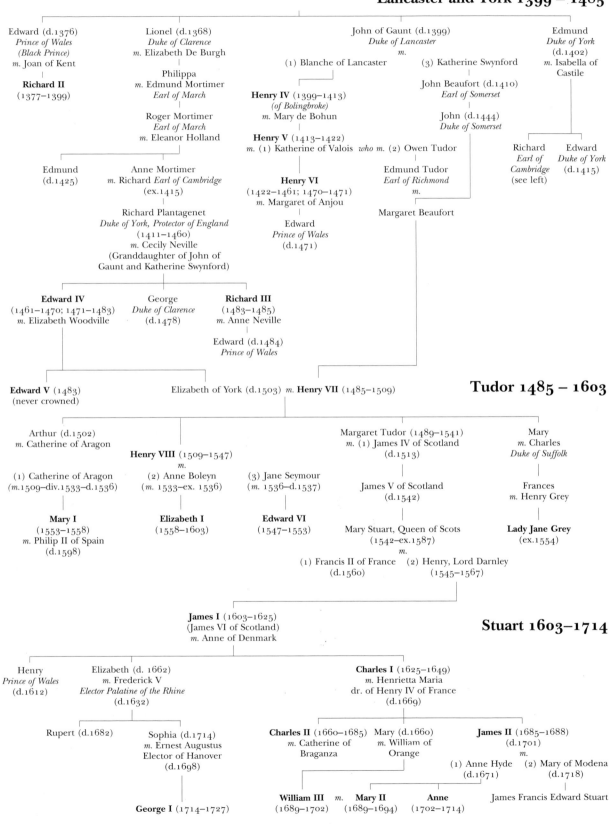

Edward (d.1376)
Prince of Wales
(Black Prince)
m. Joan of Kent

Richard II
(1377–1399)

Lionel (d.1368)
Duke of Clarence
m. Elizabeth De Burgh

Philippa
m. Edmund Mortimer
Earl of March

Roger Mortimer
Earl of March
m. Eleanor Holland

Edmund
(d.1425)

Anne Mortimer
m. Richard *Earl of Cambridge*
(ex.1415)

Richard Plantagenet
Duke of York, Protector of England
(1411–1460)
m. Cecily Neville
(Granddaughter of John of
Gaunt and Katherine Swynford)

John of Gaunt (d.1399)
Duke of Lancaster
m.

(1) Blanche of Lancaster   (3) Katherine Swynford

Henry IV (1399–1413)
(of Bolingbroke)
m. Mary de Bohun

Henry V (1413–1422)
m. (1) Katherine of Valois *who m.* (2) Owen Tudor

Henry VI
(1422–1461; 1470–1471)
m. Margaret of Anjou

Edward
Prince of Wales
(d.1471)

John Beaufort (d.1410)
Earl of Somerset

John (d.1444)
Duke of Somerset

Edmund Tudor
Earl of Richmond
m.

Margaret Beaufort

Edmund
Duke of York
(d.1402)
m. Isabella of
Castile

Richard
Earl of
Cambridge
(see left)

Edward
Duke of York
(d.1415)

Edward IV
(1461–1470; 1471–1483)
m. Elizabeth Woodville

George
Duke of Clarence
(d.1478)

Richard III
(1483–1485)
m. Anne Neville

Edward (d.1484)
Prince of Wales

Tudor 1485 – 1603

Edward V (1483)
(never crowned)

Elizabeth of York (d.1503) *m.* **Henry VII** (1485–1509)

Arthur (d.1502)
m. Catherine of Aragon

(1) Catherine of Aragon
(*m.*1509–div.1533–d.1536)

Mary I
(1553–1558)
m. Philip II of Spain
(d.1598)

Henry VIII (1509–1547)
m.

(2) Anne Boleyn
(*m.* 1533–ex. 1536)

Elizabeth I
(1558–1603)

(3) Jane Seymour
(*m.* 1536–d.1537)

Edward VI
(1547–1553)

Margaret Tudor (1489–1541)
m. (1) James IV of Scotland
(d.1513)

James V of Scotland
(d.1542)

Mary Stuart, Queen of Scots
(1542–ex.1587)
m.
(1) Francis II of France   (2) Henry, Lord Darnley
(d.1560)   (1545–1567)

Mary
m. Charles
Duke of Suffolk

Frances
m. Henry Grey

Lady Jane Grey
(ex.1554)

Stuart 1603–1714

James I (1603–1625)
(James VI of Scotland)
m. Anne of Denmark

Henry
Prince of Wales
(d.1612)

Elizabeth (d. 1662)
m. Frederick V
Elector Palatine of the Rhine
(d.1632)

Charles I (1625–1649)
m. Henrietta Maria
dr. of Henry IV of France
(d.1669)

Rupert (d.1682)

Sophia (d.1714)
m. Ernest Augustus
Elector of Hanover
(d.1698)

George I (1714–1727)

Charles II (1660–1685)
m. Catherine of
Braganza

Mary (d.1660)
m. William of
Orange

William III   *m.*   **Mary II**
(1689–1702)   (1689–1694)

James II (1685–1688)
(d.1701)
m.
(1) Anne Hyde   (2) Mary of Modena
(d.1671)   (d.1718)

Anne
(1702–1714)

James Francis Edward Stuart

Hanoverian 1714 – 1901

George I (1714–1727)
m. Sophia Dorothea of Brunswick-Zelle

George II (1727–1760)
m. Caroline of Brandenburg-Anspach

Frederick Prince of Wales (d.1751)
m. Augusta of Saxe-Gotha-Altenburg

George III (1760–1820)
m. Sophia Charlotte of Mecklenberg-Strelitz

Mary II (1689–1694)
m.
William III (1689–1702)
(son of Mary and William
of Orange)
(ruled alone from 1694)

Anne (1702–1714)
m.
George of Denmark
(d.1708)

James Francis Edward
Stuart
(*Old Pretender*)
(d.1766)

Charles Edward
(*Young Pretender*)
(d.1788)

George IV
(Regent from 1811
King 1820–1830)
m. Caroline of
Brunswick-Wölfenbuttel

Charlotte (d.1817)

Frederick
Duke of York
(d.1827)

William IV (1830–1837)
Duke of Clarence
m.
Adelaide of
Saxe-Meiningen

Edward
Duke of Kent
(d.1820)
m. Victoria of Saxe-Coburg

Ernest Augustus
King of Hanover
(d.1851)

Adolphus
Duke of Cambridge
(d.1850)

Victoria (1837–1901)
m. Albert of Saxe-Coburg-Gotha
Created Prince Consort 1857 (d.1861)

Saxe-Coburg & Windsor from 1901

Victoria (d.1901)
m. Frederick III
Emperor of Germany

Wilhelm II (d.1951)
The Kaiser

Edward VII (1901–1910)
m. Alexandra of Denmark

George V (1910–1936)
Duke of York
m. Mary of Teck

Alice (d.1878)
m. Louis IV of Hesse

Victoria (d.1950)
m. Louis of Battenberg

Alice of Battenberg (d.1969)
m. Prince Andrew of Greece

Alix of Hesse
m. Nicholas II of Russia
(both ex. 1918)

Edward VIII
Duke of Windsor (1936 Abdicated)
m. Wallis Simpson

George VI (1936–1952)
Duke of York
m. Lady Elizabeth Bowes-Lyon

Philip
(*later Duke of Edinburgh*)

Elizabeth II (1952–)
m. HRH Prince Philip
Duke of Edinburgh

Margaret
m. Antony Armstrong-Jones
1st Earl of Snowdon

Charles
Prince of Wales
m. Lady Diana Spencer
(d.1997)

William   Henry

Anne
Princess Royal
m.(1) Mark Phillips
m.(2) Timothy Laurence

Andrew
Duke of York
m. Sarah Ferguson

Edward
Earl of Wessex
m. Sophie Rhys-Jones

David
Viscount Linley
m. Serena Stanhope

Lady Sarah
Armstrong-Jones
m. Daniel Chatto

KINGS AND QUEENS OF SCOTLAND

❖

MAC ALPINE

843–58	Kenneth I
858–62	Donald I
862–77	Constantine I
877–78	Aedh
878–89	Eocha
889–900	Donald II
900–43	Constantine II
943–54	Malcolm I
954–62	Indulf
962–66	Duff
966–71	Colin
971–95	Kenneth II
995–97	Constantine III
997–1005	Kenneth III
1005–34	Malcolm II
1034–40	Duncan I
1040–57	Macbeth
1058	Luiach

CANMORE

1057–93	Malcolm III
1093	Donald Bane
1094	Duncan II
1094–97	Donald Bane
1097–1107	Edgar
1107–24	Alexander I
1124–53	David I
1153–65	Malcolm IV
1165–1214	William I
1214–49	Alexander II
1249–86	Alexander III
1286–90	Margaret
1290–92	No king

BALLIOL

1292–96	John Balliol
1296–1306	No king

BRUCE

1306–29	Robert I
1329–71	David II

STUART

1371–90	Robert II
1390–1406	Robert III
1406–19	Regent Albany
1419–24	Regent Murdoch
1424–37	James I
1437–60	James II
1460–88	James III
1488–1513	James IV
1513–42	James V
1542–67	Mary
1567–1625	JamesVI

In 1603 James VI became King of England, Wales and Ireland. From 1603 onwards the rulers of Scotland are the same as the rulers of England and Wales.

PRIME MINISTERS 1721–2001

❖

1721	Sir Robert Walpole
1741	Earl of Wilmington
1743	Henry Pelham
1754	Duke of Newcastle
1756	Duke of Devonshire
1757	Duke of Newcastle
1762	Earl of Bute
1763	George Grenville
1765	Marquess of Rockingham
1766	Earl of Chatham
1768	Duke of Grafton
1770	Lord North
1782	Marquess of Rockingham
1782	Earl of Shelburne
1783	Duke of Portland
1783	William Pitt
1801	Henry Addington
1804	William Pitt
1806	William Wyndham Grenville
1807	Duke of Portland
1809	Spencer Perceval
1812	Earl of Liverpool
1827	George Canning
1827	Viscount Goderich
1828	Duke of Wellington
1830	Earl Grey

1834	Viscount Melbourne
1834	Duke of Wellington
1834	Sir Robert Peel
1835	Viscount Melbourne
1841	Sir Robert Peel
1846	Lord John Russell
1852	Earl of Derby
1852	Earl of Aberdeen
1855	Viscount Palmerston
1858	Earl of Derby
1859	Viscount Palmerston
1865	Earl Russell
1866	Earl of Derby
1868	Benjamin Disraeli
1868	William Ewart Gladstone
1874	Benjamin Disraeli
1880	William Ewart Gladstone
1885	Marquess of Salisbury
1886	William Ewart Gladstone
1886	Marquess of Salisbury
1892	William Ewart Gladstone
1894	Earl of Rosebery
1895	Marquess of Salisbury
1902	Arthur James Balfour
1905	Sir Henry Campbell-Bannerman

1908	Herbert Henry Asquith
1916	David Lloyd George
1922	Andrew Bonar Law
1923	Stanley Baldwin
1924	James Ramsay MacDonald
1924	Stanley Baldwin
1929	James Ramsay MacDonald
1935	Stanley Baldwin
1937	Neville Chamberlain
1940	Winston Churchill
1945	Clement Attlee
1951	Winston Churchill
1955	Sir Anthony Eden
1957	Harold Macmillan
1963	Sir Alec Douglas-Home
1964	Harold Wilson
1970	Edward Heath
1974	Harold Wilson
1976	James Callaghan
1979	Margaret Thatcher
1990	John Major
1997	Tony Blair

INDEX

❖

ACKNOWLEDGEMENTS

p2 Nat. Maritime Museum, London; p6 Bruce Coleman Ltd; p8 Natural History Museum, London; p9c Kate Brimscombe/ The Independent; p10cl Nat. Museum of Wales, b & p11 British Museum; p12 Nat. Museum of Wales; p13t BM; p15 FLPA; p17t & b Historic Scotland; p18 English Heritage; p20 Somerset Levels Project; p21 BM; p22 EH; p23t John Scarry, b Office of Public Works, Dublin; p24t Mick Sharp, b Devizes Museum; pp25-29 EH; p30obl Michael Jenner; p31-5t Mick Sharp; p31c Ulster Museum; p32 Bill Marsden for Humberside County Council; p33 BM; p36t Nationalmuseet, Copenhagen, b Michael Jenner; pp37-8 BM; p39 AKG London; p40 BM; pp41, 42-3t EH; p42b Michael Jenner; pp43b, 46t Colchester Museums; pp45t, b, 46b EH; p47 BM; pp49, 50 EH; p53 Dominic Powlesland; p54 British Library (Beowulf); pp55, 56 BM; p57 Nat. Museum of Ireland; p58-9b Michael Jenner; p59 BL (Lindisfarne Gospel); p60 BM; p61 ET; p62 EH; p63 Ashmolean Museum, Oxford; p64 BL (Ms.Cott.Tib. B v pt1., f40v); p65l Michael Jenner, r Charles Tait; pp66, 67 York Archaeological Trust;

The illustrations are by: Richard Berridge/ Specs Art p9; Mike Codd p12-13, p20; Mel Wright p19.

All maps are by Hardlines, Charlbury, Oxfordshire.

Abbreviations:
BL = British Library; BM = British Museum; CCC = Corpus Christi College; EH = English Heritage; ET = E. T. Archive; IWM = Imperial War Museum; NG = National Gallery, London; NPG = National Portrait Gallery, London; V & A = Victoria & Albert Museum, London; W & N = Weidenfeld & Nicolson Archives